THE
GROWTH
MINDSET
PLAYBOOK

THE
GROWTH
MINDSET
PLAYBOOK

A Teacher's Guide to Promoting Student Success

Annie Brock and Heather Hundley

Ulysses Press

Published in the United States by:
Ulysses Press
P.O. Box 3440
Berkeley, CA 94703
www.ulyssespress.com

ISBN13: 978-1-61243-687-6
Library of Congress Control Number: 2016957513

Printed in Canada by Marquis Book Printing
10 9 8 7 6 5 4 3 2 1

Acquisitions editor: Casie Vogel
Managing editor: Claire Chun
Editor: Shayna Keyles
Proofreader: Renee Rutledge
Indexer: Sayre Van Young
Front cover and interior design: what!design @ whatweb.com
Artwork: cover © Cienpies Design/shutterstock.com; page 102 © Oxy_gen/shutterstock
    .com
Layout: Jake Flaherty

Distributed by Publishers Group West

For Jared.
In memory of Helen Moulin.

—A.B.

For Matt.
SHMILY

—H.H.

CONTENTS

INTRODUCTION: THE WARM-UP

*They call it coaching, but it is teaching. You do not
just tell them—you show them the reasons.*

—Vince Lombardi

Hey, you! Yeah, you, the super-cool teacher reading this book. We think you're pretty great. We know what you're thinking. *How can you think I'm great? You don't even know me!* Well, we do know a little something about you. You bought this book! (Or borrowed it from a friend, or checked it out from the library, or found it in a dumpster. Though we *really* hope it's not that last one.) Reading this book means that you're interested in learning new ideas and strategies to improve your teaching practice which just so happens to be a foundational skill of growth mindset. See? You're already nailing it! It's like when you get 20 points for just writing your name on the SAT. (Speaking of which, is that just a myth or the real deal?) Anyway, we know you're a good egg, because we've known bad teachers—not many, but there are a few floating around out there—and you know the one defining characteristic of a "bad" teacher? They've given up. Checked out. Taken a hard pass on self-improvement. We know you haven't given up, because you dug this book out of dumpster! Or bought it, maybe. But, no matter how you got the book, we're glad you are here, and overjoyed that you've chosen to come along on this growth mindset journey with us.

THE GROWTH MINDSET COACH

In the fall of 2016, we released *The Growth Mindset Coach*, where we took the concept of mindset as outlined in Carol Dweck's best-selling book *Mindset: The New Psychology of Success*, and applied it to the classroom. We came from different backgrounds. Heather was a long-time elementary school teacher, having taught third, first, and, most recently, kindergarten. Annie was a writer turned high school English teacher and library media specialist. But the idea of growth mindset resonated with us because of its applicability at every level. Even though our experiences in the classroom were as different as *The Cat and the Hat* and *Julius Caesar*, we realized that we shared many commonalities in our approaches to teaching. Namely, we were most successful with students when we built strong relationships, cultivated essential non-cognitive skills, and helped students see their undeniable potential to achieve academic and personal growth.

In writing *The Growth Mindset Coach*, we had the opportunity to share our teaching philosophies with educators from all over the world. We knew the power of seeing our efforts pay off inside the four walls of our own classrooms, but were not quite prepared for how rewarding it felt to hear from teachers and students we'd never met who were using, and benefiting from, ideas and lessons shared in our book. You know that feeling a teacher gets when a student masters a difficult concept after wrestling with it for a while? Of course you know the one—we teachers are *aha* moment junkies! Well, in publishing our book, we were suddenly privy to these special moments from teachers and students who hailed from cities we'd never even heard of. How gratifying it was to know that our humble work was actually making a difference! This is why we decided to follow up our first effort with a second.

The Growth Mindset Playbook might be considered a sequel to our first book, but it also has the ability to stand alone. So, if you haven't read our first book, don't worry! This book is useful for any teacher interested in promoting the beliefs and values of growth mindset in the classroom. Mindset is a powerful concept that, when used correctly, has unlimited application in schools and classrooms in every corner of the globe.

We said in our first book, and we'll say it again here, that growth mindset is not a cure-all for what is wrong with the public school system. From segregation and inequity of resources to over-testing and lack of parental involvement, we can point to any number of factors at work that depress our educational efforts. Promoting the science of mindset among today's educational shareholders certainly cannot fix these systemic issues, but we believe that it can make a difference. In Chile, for example, it was found that low-income students with a growth mindset narrowed the achievement gap between themselves and their high-socioeconomic status counterparts, while low-income students with a fixed mindset did not.[1] (We'll talk more about that study in Chapter 1.) Growth mindset has even played a role in improving children's health. Research recently revealed that among children with Type I diabetes, those with a fixed mindset had higher glucose levels than those with a growth mindset. Why? Researchers believe that when children have fixed mindsets about their health—the belief they are genetically predisposed to feel a certain way and there is nothing they can do to meaningfully change it—they are less likely to follow doctor's orders or try to maintain a healthcare regimen.[2]

There is far more work to be done in studying the implications of developing growth mindsets, but there is ample evidence that they can work in improving academic outcomes. For now, our very best advice is: Bloom where you are planted. Sometimes, the best you can do is start from where you are with what you have. What we seek to do here is give you an understanding of and strategies for teaching and developing growth mindset, along with a whole host of non-cognitive skills closely related to mindset that can help propel you and your students toward more fulfilling lives.

WHY DID WE CALL IT THE PLAYBOOK?

Head to your local soccer fields on a fall Saturday morning or the community baseball diamond on a breezy summer evening, and you'll see kids playing sports. Along with that, you'll see parents acting as coaches, fans, and sometimes even referees. They will yell out encouragements, pointers, and instructions from the stands. They will pull a kid to the side and go over a concept after a failure on the field. These adults will be doing and saying a lot of things that we don't often see when it comes to school. If a goalie lets a ball slip by into the net, you won't hear a parent say, "Well, he's just not cut out to be a goalie." Or, if a little softball player strikes out for the third time that game, you won't hear the coach say, "Oh, well. She's not meant to get a hit." More often than not, you will hear adults engaging in the language of growth mindset:

"You can do it!"

"Keep your eye on the ball!"

"You'll get it next time!"

But when it comes to schoolwork, adults all too often invoke the kind of learning stereotypes and fixed-mindset thinking they wouldn't be caught dead spouting on the playing field. You'll never hear a parent yell out, "I stunk at pitching too, son. Just give up now!" while watching their child on the field. No way!

Growth mindset is a way of being, a way of approaching problems, and a way of picking yourself up when you fall. The embodiment of growth mindset manifests in all sorts of non-cognitive characteristics: grit, tenacity, persistence, resilience, and a host of other valuable qualities that emerge when children begin to understand that they have the power to achieve anything, as long as they are willing to work for it. These are qualities that parents value on the sports field; in fact, the language of growth mindset is embedded in the way we coach our children. But when it comes to school, parents become more like cognitive cheerleaders. Instead of encouraging grit and resilience like they would in the sporting arena, they adopt a belief that success at school is about innate intellectualism, natural ability, genetics, or talent. Parents and coaches of youth sports don't stress winning at all costs; in fact, they often take care to discourage that kind of attitude. But when it comes to school, all that goes out the window and the focus shifts to good grades, high test scores, and, in essence, winning in the classroom.

WHAT YOU'LL FIND IN THE BOOK

In this book, we will share more strategies, tips, ideas, and research that will help you understand mindset and how it can contribute to positive outcomes for your students. Many of the names and identifying details in this book have been changed to protect the students and teachers with whom we have worked.

Additionally, our teaching experiences, while rich and fulfilling, have been in mostly rural Title I schools, with predominately white and Native American populations. Though our content areas, grade levels, and student demographics may differ from those in our readers' experiences, we try to appeal to what is common among our students. Most of what we write about has more to do with the human condition than the school condition. Why? Because we believe that our job is to prepare students for life, which means we must instill in them all the things that make life purposeful, joyful, and extraordinary. And that has to start with fostering in our students the authentic belief that they are the masters of their own destiny, that the choices they make each day compound in incredible ways, and that there are no limitations on what they might achieve in this life.

In pursuit of that goal, we won't be talking much about the cognitive aspect of teaching, except to say that we believe strong, holistic education includes rigorous academic preparation rooted in sound pedagogy. It would be impossible to fully realize the power of teaching growth mindset to your students if they did not have opportunities to utilize it in an environment that offers challenging work, well-designed curriculum, and high-quality instruction.

And while curriculum and pedagogy are critical to a quality education, equally important are the non-cognitive skills our students are learning in school. It's easy to get wrapped up in the idea that test scores automatically lead to achievement, but the research does not bear that out. In fact, as economist James Heckman wrote in his book *Inequality in America: What Role for Human Capital Policies?*, "Numerous instances can be cited of people with high IQs who fail to achieve success in life because they lacked self-discipline and of people with low IQs who succeeded by virtue of persistence, reliability, and self-discipline."[3] If you have spent any amount of time teaching, you likely have anecdotal evidence to support Heckman's contention. We've all encountered the would-be high-achieving student completely lacking in motivation, or the

Little-Engine-Who-Could student who may struggle to master concepts, but succeeds with a winning combination of pluck and determination.

Studies have shown that consistency and self-discipline are linked with academic achievement and success later in life. But it's difficult to help students wrap their heads around the notion that the small choices they are making today—in 6th grade math, for example—have long-term implications on their future success. The explicit teaching of non-cognitive skills is crucial in this regard. The Stanford University Project for Education Research that Scales (PERTS), a lab that has extensively researched growth mindset, conducted a study that revealed that when students are explicitly taught about growth mindset and how they learn, along with why and how what they are learning today will help them achieve their unique future goals, their academic motivation increases and they experience more positive results compared to students who don't receive the same explicit instruction.[4]

This study reinforces our belief in a holistic education that includes non-cognitive instruction. Viewing each student as a whole person who uniquely connects with information and the world is critical in creating a learning environment that will serve students even after they leave the classroom. When a student learns about mindsets, they gain an understanding of their power in shaping their own future. Putting growth mindset into practice manifests in a host of skills, abilities, and experiences, from developing grit and resilience to improving relationships and increasing self-regulation. When students' growth mindsets emerge, they begin to experience a transformation of the whole self. This is why teaching mindset isn't just about giving students information about how they learn or praising students' effort: Being a growth-oriented teacher means developing your own growth mindset and modeling it for students in an authentic way. Your example will empower students to change their own beliefs. They will start viewing failures as opportunities for improvement, feeling emboldened rather than intimidated by challenges, and growing in ways they never thought possible.

A MINDSET REFRESHER

If you haven't heard about mindsets before now, we recommend adding Carol Dweck's book, *Mindset: The New Psychology of Success*, to your reading list right away. As a young researcher in the 1970s, Dweck studied how students coped with failure. In the course of her work, she realized that some students thrived in the face of difficult challenges, while others shut down completely. Moreover, the students who were willing to embrace a challenge and grapple with failure had better outcomes than the students who engaged in avoidance tactics when they encountered a struggle in their learning. She quickly shifted the focus of her work to study the phenomenon she was witnessing, and began seeing it everywhere—in education, parenting, business, and even sports. Eventually, she came up with a name for it: mindset.

In her research and observations, Dweck identified two separate mindsets common in her subjects: fixed mindset and growth mindset.

> **FIXED MINDSET:** The belief that people are born with a fixed amount of intelligence and ability. People operating in the fixed mindset are prone to avoiding challenges and failures, thereby robbing themselves of a life rich in experience and learning.[5]

> **GROWTH MINDSET:** The belief that with practice, perseverance, and effort, people have limitless potential to learn and grow. People operating in the growth mindset take on challenges with the understanding that making mistakes and failing are essential to growth.[6]

A person with a fixed mindset believes that people are born with a fixed set of intelligences, skills, and talents. Often, when faced with a challenging situation, those with a fixed mindset work very hard to avoid failing or looking stupid, robbing themselves of rich life experiences. Conversely, people with a growth mindset generally believe that with practice, perseverance, and effort, they have unlimited potential to learn and grow. In this mindset, intelligence, skill, and talent are in infinite supply, if one is willing to work for them. People with growth mindsets are more inclined to tackle challenges, and believe making mistakes and overcoming obstacles are integral to the process of growth.

We think it is important to have an understanding of which of the mindsets—fixed or growth—is your predominant mindset. If you've never taken a mindset assessment, it's easy. Just put a check next to the statements that best describe your beliefs.

1. _____ There are some things I am just not good at.

2. _____ I don't mind failing. It's a chance to learn.

3. _____ When others do better than me, it makes me feel inferior.

4. _____ I like trying new things, even if it means getting out of my comfort zone.

5. _____ It makes me feel successful when I show others I'm good at things.

6. _____ When other people succeed, I feel inspired.

7. _____ I feel good when I can do something others around me cannot.

8. _____ It is possible to change how intelligent you are.

9. _____ I think people are born with a certain amount of intelligence and they can't do much to change that.

10._____ Feeling frustrated makes me want to try harder.

In this assessment, the odd-numbered statements (1, 3, 5, 7, 9) are common attitudes of someone operating in a fixed mindset, while the even-numbered statements (2, 4, 6, 8, 10) are common of a person operating in a growth mindset. It's important to remember there are no right and wrong answers here; understanding your predominant mindset is simply the first step in developing a growth-oriented classroom. Most likely, you are a mixture of the mindsets. Some tasks you probably approach with a growth mindset, while taking on others might trigger your fixed mindset. Regardless of your starting point, here's what we know: Your ability to grow and change in this regard depends on the amount of work you're willing to do. If you're ready to put in the work to become an authentic growth-mindset teacher, then we have no doubt you can achieve it.

MORE ABOUT THE MINDSETS

Dweck identified five key situations in which mindset makes a big difference: challenges, obstacles, effort, criticism, and success of others.[7] She examined the actions of people experiencing these situations and concluded that how a person approaches a given situation—with a fixed mindset or growth mindset—significantly influences the outcome. For a person operating in the fixed mindset, the goal is most often to appear smart and capable and to avoid embarrassment or failure, whereas in the growth mindset, a person's situational responses are rooted in a desire to grow and develop, regardless of the potential for failure. Let's look at some typical fixed- and growth-mindset responses to each of the five situations Dweck defined.

SITUATION	FIXED MINDSET	GROWTH MINDSET
Challenges	Challenges are avoided to maintain the appearance of intelligence and capability.	Challenges are embraced, demonstrating a desire to learn and grow.
Obstacles	Giving up in the face of obstacles and setbacks is a common response in the fixed mindset.	Showing grit and resilience in the face of obstacles and setbacks is a common response in the growth mindset.
Effort	Putting in effort is viewed as a negative trait; if you're good at it, you shouldn't have to try hard.	Putting in effort and working hard are critical to paving the way to achievement and success.
Criticism	Negative feedback, regardless of how constructive, is ignored. It's often viewed as a personal attack.	Criticism isn't a personal attack, it's a tool for providing important feedback that can aid in learning and growth.
Success of others	The success of others is viewed as a threat and evokes feelings of insecurity or vulnerability.	The success of other people can be a source of inspiration and education.

THE MINDSETS AT SCHOOL

Now that you have an understanding of the two mindsets, let's examine how they might be at play in your school or classroom. Below, you'll find hypothetical examples of self-talk from the fixed- and growth-mindset perspectives; note how they have very different views of the same situations.

FIXED MINDSET	GROWTH MINDSET
My administrator gave me a bad review. He knows nothing about what I do in class all day. He just hates me.	I need to follow up on the "needs improvement" areas of my review with specific questions. Maybe my administrator can point me to resources to help improve these areas of my teaching.
Megan is bad at math. It's just not something she's good at.	How can I teach Megan math in a way that connects her to the material?
Jay can do the work, but he's not doing it. He's just lazy.	I know Jay can do the work, but he's not doing it. I need to reexamine my approach and figure out how to engage him.
Mr. Jones gets all the teaching awards and accolades because he is a total suck-up and glory-seeker.	Mr. Jones gets recognized often for his teaching. I should observe him to see if I can apply some of his strategies to my own practice.
My students ruined this lesson; they just refused to cooperate.	My students didn't connect with this lesson. How could I make it more engaging for them?
This class is filled with bad kids. I've heard they are completely unteachable.	I will approach this class taking each individual student into account. All students can be taught. It's just a matter of finding the right approach.
Dara's parents obviously don't value education. She'll never go anywhere with a family like that.	I believe Dara's parents want what is best for her; how can I give them the tools they need to support her in a positive way?
Carl has a bad attitude and is completely checked out; he has no hope of graduating.	I should ask Carl to write down his future goals, and help him see how his choices now will make a difference.
My students performed poorly on this test; obviously they weren't listening.	My students performed poorly on this test; obviously I need to reteach the material in a way they will understand.

Hopefully, you're beginning to see a pattern. The fixed-mindset teacher approaches situations as unchangeable, and a difficult situation is viewed as a personal attack or as someone else's fault. Now, juxtapose that teacher's approach with the inner monologue of a growth-mindset teacher. The growth-mindset teacher handles these same situations with a completely different point of view. Compared to the fixed-mindset teacher, who is quick to give up and lay the blame at the foot of another, the growth-mindset teacher seeks to understand the problem and find a way to solve it. When a lesson or assignment fails in the classroom, the fixed-mindset teacher starts looking for someone to blame, while the growth-mindset teacher is too busy heading back to the drawing board to bother with finger pointing. When an administrator suggests a constructive change to teaching style, the fixed-mindset teacher takes the criticism personally or tries to deflect it altogether, while the growth-mindset teacher values feedback—even critical feedback—as an essential part of teaching and a stepping stone toward improvement.

Take a week to examine your mindset in the classroom. Listen to both your inner monologue and the words you speak aloud. How often are you using your growth mindset? What triggers your fixed mindset? Pay special attention to how and when your mindsets emerge. Having a good understanding of your own mindset is crucial to your success or failure in teaching it to others. When your students have a strong role model, they will be more likely to exhibit growth-mindset characteristics.

BEWARE THE FALSE GROWTH MINDSET

Dweck has warned, since the release and subsequent success of her book, of something she calls the "false growth mindset."[8] As her mindset theory grew in popularity, Dweck noticed a startling trend: an oversimplification of what growth mindset is and how to develop it in young people. Dweck saw teachers who were praising students for effort, even when the effort resulted in no real achievement. This hollow praise actually counters growth mindset, and is more akin to the self-esteem frenzy that Dweck saw as the antithesis of her mindset movement.

While overpraising for effort is problematic, more so is the belief that lack of growth mindset is to blame for systemic issues in education. As an example, in a survey of white college students it was found that students often viewed non-white peers as failing to achieve success because of a lack of effort. This short-sighted perspective fails to take into account the various educational inequities non-white students experience, and demonstrates why it's important to view growth mindset not as an end-all-be-all key to success, but rather through a nuanced lens.[9]

If you're coming into this book with the notion that growth mindset is all about praising kids for effort or that it can cure all that ails the American public school system, you will likely be disappointed. While Dweck's theory is simple to understand, growth mindset is difficult for anyone, including us, to practice all the time, or even a majority of the time. And inspiring students to change their mindsets? That's a big job! Even when kids do demonstrate a growth mindset, there are many other hurdles to success in school, particularly for those students who have been historically underserved or subject to discriminatory practices. Dweck has also seen another kind of "false growth mindset"—those who claim to have an unimpeachable growth mindset all the time. It just can't be true.

We all have a mixture of growth and fixed mindsets. And teachers who claim a growth mindset but model a fixed mindset in the classroom can be particularly detrimental. It's better to admit to yourself and your students that all people possess a unique mixture of growth and fixed mindsets that emerge in different environments and situations. Be honest with yourself and others when you encounter a fixed-mindset trigger, and model how to work through situations that challenge your growth mindset. Modeling your own struggles with mindset shows your students that you are a whole, complex person with strengths and weaknesses, just as they are. Simply, you can't just talk the talk, you've got to walk the walk. Claiming growth-mindset mastery is a big red flag that you don't get it, yet. The ability to understand what triggers your fixed mindset and experiment with strategies to handle those tricky situations is the true mark of a growth mindset. Embracing your strengths and giving yourself grace as you work through your weaknesses sets a powerful example for your students. It will help students understand their own complexity as individuals experiencing the world and encourage them to give themselves grace as they rise and fall.

GAME ON

In this book, we delve into many concepts and ideas that are not specifically about mindset. But we've learned that mindset is present in virtually every part of our lives. As we seek to develop ourselves and our students on both cognitive and non-cognitive levels, utilizing growth mindset serves as a powerful tool. In this book, we'll talk about some of those tricky situations we run into at school and how we can use the principles of growth mindset and related strategies to successfully navigate them, all while empowering students, parents, and colleagues through your example. We'll talk about building relationships, navigating discipline, overcoming setbacks, and challenging conventional thinking, along with a host of other school-day issues, and how approaching these situations with a growth mindset leads to better outcomes for all of us. Each time you step into your classroom, it's game on. This is your playbook, Coach; it's game time!

1

PLAY 1: THE BEST WE CAN BE

I don't know what lies around the bend, but

I'm going to believe that the best does.

—Lucy Maud Montgomery, *Anne of Green Gables*

Here's the bad news. Yep, we're going to tell you the bad news first, mainly because you have to know what the problem is before you go about figuring out how to tackle it. So, here it goes: A lot of kids have lost hope. They have lost hope in themselves, they have lost hope in their futures, and they have lost hope in you, their teachers. It's our job to figure out how to get them to hope again. We know that's an awfully big challenge, and you probably aren't getting paid much to get it done. But we also know there's a reason you got into the business of teaching kids, and it sure as heck wasn't for the money (or the cafeteria food). At your core, you are a person who believes in the very best of people; in fact, you've dedicated your life to helping people become the best versions of themselves. We know this business can be tough sometimes, and it's easy to get bogged down by bureaucracy and forget what we're here for: the kids. If the kids are saying they've lost hope, then it's our job to help them find it again. And if anyone can do it, it's you!

LOSING HOPE

In 2015, Gallup conducted its annual student poll, which asks all sorts of questions about the school experience. The poll also includes the "Hope Index," which has survey items that attempt to measure non-cognitive attributes of the educational experience of American students. The results were troubling. Just over 60 percent of the one million fifth through twelfth graders surveyed strongly agreed with the statement, "I have a great future ahead of me." If you think it's bad that 40 percent of our students don't believe in a fantastic future for themselves, hold on, because it gets worse! Only 33 percent of students strongly agreed with the statement, "I have a mentor who encourages my development."[10] How can that be? Two-thirds of American students surveyed cannot readily identify an adult who encourages their growth?

For those of us in the business of growth mindset, those numbers aren't good. Before many students even leave school, they have conceived of an unsuccessful future for themselves. Why? Perhaps because so few students report having an encouraging, supportive adult presence in their lives.

Here are two more results from the Gallup survey: Only half of students responded that they strongly agreed with the statement, "I can think of many ways to get good grades." And just 35 percent responded they strongly agreed with the statement, "I can find many ways around problems." So let's review: Not only are students reporting they cannot find adults who they consider encouraging mentors and that they do not believe in their potential for future success, but a majority of them are admitting to lacking a basic belief in their ability to make good grades and solve problems. It's hard to make sense of this data, because we know that teachers all across this nation show up to school every day and put everything they have into developing, nurturing, and empowering their students. We also know that our classrooms are filled with curious, capable students with limitless potential. So where is the disconnect?

One view might be that this hopelessness students are reporting is a manifestation of fixed mindsets. If students buy into the idea that they can't make good grades, they can't solve problems, no one really cares, and it doesn't matter because they're not going to have a successful future anyway, they insulate themselves against the possibility of future disappointment and failure. These are the hallmarks of a fixed mindset. The fixed mindset is convincing yourself that your options are limited and your shortcomings are either genetically or environmentally predetermined.

"Some of you might not have those advantages," said former President Barack Obama in a speech to students at Wakefield High School in Arlington, Virginia. "Maybe you don't have adults in your life who give you the support that you need. Maybe someone in your family has lost their job, and there's not enough money to go around. Maybe you live in a neighborhood where you don't feel safe, or have friends who are pressuring you to do things you know aren't right. But at the end of the day, the circumstances of your life, what you look like, where you come from, how much money you have, what you've got going on at home… That's no excuse for not trying. Where you are right now doesn't have to determine where you'll end up. No one's written your destiny for you. Here in America, you write your own destiny. You make your own future."[11]

Admitting to having potential and high hopes for the future takes courage. It takes a growth mindset. Growth mindset isn't easy, especially in the difficult circumstances many of today's students find themselves facing each day. It means tackling challenges head on, persevering through setbacks, and having an unwavering belief in your ability to succeed.

THE GROWTH MINDSET FACTOR

Growth-mindset research suggests that teaching mindset can make a difference, especially for students feeling this hopelessness. Once a person understands their own power to shape their future through dedicated practice, hard work, and effort, it's a game changer. Dweck often tells a story of teaching a group of young students about their ability to grow their own brain through practice and effort. She remembers one boy raising his hand and asking: "You mean, I don't have to be dumb?"[12]

Not only has teaching kids about growth mindset proven to increase academic outcomes, but students who have a growth mindset find school less threatening and view it as an exciting place to learn and grow. Moreover, student outcomes increase when teachers model growth mindset and offer explicit instruction on the mindsets and how the brain can grow and change over time.[13]

Dweck's research suggests that when students adopt the growth mindset, their achievement increases, along with their motivation. Recent research Dweck and her colleagues conducted in 2014 in Chile revealed that students who indicated a strong growth mindset, regardless of their socioeconomic status, had better academic outcomes than students who had strong fixed mindsets, and that growth-mindset students from low-income backgrounds fared better academically than economically privileged students with fixed mindsets.[14] This indicates the potential for closing achievement gaps through growth-mindset instruction.

Student mindsets are heavily influenced by messages from their environments. A growth-mindset teacher can go far in modeling mindset for students, helping them arrive at the understanding that their intelligence, skills, and abilities are not fixed, and that with effort and perseverance they can make great improvements in any area. When students' fixed mindsets are transformed to growth mindsets, as Dweck reports, student outcomes improve, and students who demonstrate a growth mindset outperform their fixed-mindset peers.

It appears that schools are getting the message that developing mindsets can make a difference in student achievement. In a national study of K–12 teachers conducted by the Education Week Research Center, over half of teachers reported receiving formal training on the topic of growth mindset and made efforts to integrate mindset in their classrooms. When done correctly, cultivating a growth-oriented learning environment can empower students to engage in challenging work, rise up after failure, and realize their potential to succeed in all areas of education. Unfortunately, some research has suggested that many teachers attempting to integrate growth mindset in the classroom may have "critical misunderstandings" about the process, leading to surprisingly low success rates.[15]

UNDERWHELMING RESULTS

Researcher John Hattie reported that, despite Carol Dweck's body of evidence to the contrary, his analysis indicated that teaching growth and fixed mindset had a very low effect size, a measurement of how well an intervention worked according to collected data, in student outcomes. In other words, the results for the mindset intervention were underwhelming. How can this be? Dweck and her colleagues have reams of data indicating the positive nature of the growth-mindset intervention. All the data points to growth-mindset integration in the classroom having positive impacts on students, and here is one of the foremost education researchers telling us that the numbers from the classroom didn't bear out Dweck's research results.

Peter DeWitt, a colleague of Hattie, writes in *Education Week* that Hattie posited, based on his meta-analysis, that the effect size of mindset interventions was low not because of the mindsets of the students, but rather the mindsets of the teachers. That's right. Teaching about growth mindset didn't make a lick of difference if the teacher had a fixed mindset. Teachers seemed not to be putting their money where their mouths were. They were teaching growth mindset but not exhibiting it. For those who were both teaching and modeling growth mindset, Hattie suggested, the effect sizes were more profound. DeWitt points to several factors that may contribute to sending fixed-mindset messaging to students, like over-testing, ability grouping, and unnecessary intervention services.

"We do not have a crystal ball," DeWitt wrote, "and we shouldn't treat students who struggle like they will struggle for the rest of their lives. It's like a self-fulfilling prophecy."[16]

Hattie argues that while there is potential for a larger effect size in mindset interventions, as long as teachers have a fixed mindset, that potential will not be realized. Think of it like that familiar flight-attendant lecture at the beginning of every flight: You must put your own oxygen mask on first before trying to help others. If the teacher hasn't truly embraced the growth mindset, they will continue sending fixed-mindset messages, consciously or otherwise, to the students in their classrooms, and that's not going to help anyone.

WHAT MATTERS MOST

Nadia Lopez, Principal of Mott Hall Bridges Academy, illustrates Hattie's point with an anecdote in her book *The Bridge to Brilliance*. In the book, she writes that in a staff meeting one day, she asked teachers to create a list describing a special education student who was experiencing some struggles in school. The teachers collaborated on a list that featured things like, "writes slow," "never completes tasks on time," "lacks motivation," and "easily distracted." The list ultimately totaled 21 itemized characteristics, and all were negative.

Then Lopez asked the two paraprofessionals tasked with working with the same student to make a list describing him. Their list featured things like, "concerned about others," "helpful," "loves to volunteer," and "neat handwriting." Twelve items on the list, and all were positive. What could account for the differences in the two lists? Lopez argues that the traditional dynamics of the education system force teachers to focus on the curriculum instead of the whole child. The paraprofessionals, on the other hand, are focused on supporting the student.[17] The system is set up in such a way that the teacher zones in on the child's weaknesses as problems to be corrected, while the paraprofessional focuses on the student's strengths in an effort to help him use his best attributes to get the work done.

Sometimes teachers become so enveloped in the process of teaching—the curriculum, the testing, the outcomes—that they forget to focus on what matters most: the students. The growth-mindset teacher must have a true assessment of his or her students, both their assets and their deficits. Perhaps this is why Hattie's research indicated a lower effect size than one might expect in the growth-mindset interventions. If teachers aren't displaying an authentic growth mindset, they can't effectively communicate the value of it to students. Remember, you have to put your oxygen mask on first if you want to have any hope of helping others.

YOUR MINDSET

In the Introduction, you did a mindset assessment, and it is very likely that you exhibited characteristics of both a growth and fixed mindset. You may have discovered some mindset triggers, like dealing with a toxic colleague or a week of assessment testing, that send you spiraling into a fixed mindset. It's important to be aware of these triggers. Think about a typical day for you at school. What feeds your growth mindset? Maybe it's a student having an important breakthrough or an administrator approving your request to go to a conference. And what feeds your fixed mindset? Maybe it's your diligently planned lesson falling short of expectations or a colleague making a critical comment about your teaching. In knowing what feeds your growth mindset, you can seek out opportunities and use strategies that empower you. Equally important, understanding your fixed-mindset triggers can help you plan for them and work out strategies to help you deal with managing your mindset or eliminating those triggers from your day, when possible.

Something that bolsters my growth mindset is…

1. _____

2. _____

3. _____

Something that triggers my fixed mindset is…

1. _____

2. _____

3. _____

As you begin to understand your own triggers and motivators, share those with students and have them come up with their own lists. Here's a mini-lesson for teaching students how to recognize situations that trigger their fixed mindsets, and how they can develop strategies to take control of those situations in a positive way.

RESPONDING TO FIXED-MINDSET TRIGGERS
MINI-LESSON

LEARNING OBJECTIVE

At the end of the lesson, students will be able to:

- identify their personal fixed-mindset triggers

- formulate responses that engage growth-oriented self-talk and strategies

RESOURCES AND MATERIALS

- Note cards

- Pencil

METHOD

Note: You may first want to share personal fixed-mindset triggers and strategies for how to go about changing your self-talk, as well as any struggles you have encountered as you work to foster growth-mindset thinking. Students need to have a basic understanding of the mindsets and how they impact learning before beginning this lesson.

First, pass out prepared fixed- and growth-mindset statements on note cards to each student. Create a class T-chart using the growth and fixed statements. Ask your students to place their note card statements under the fixed or growth category. Provide students an opportunity to share and rationalize their thinking with their peers.

You can use these statements for your cards, or create your own.

FIXED MINDSET	GROWTH MINDSET
When I have to ask for help or get called on in class, I get anxious and feel like people will think I'm not smart.	The question I have is likely the same question someone else in class may have. It's important for me to ask so I can better understand what I am learning.

FIXED MINDSET	GROWTH MINDSET
My teacher gave me a low score on my presentation. I knew I couldn't do the work because I'm just not creative. There is no way I am revising it for a better score.	My score wasn't as good as I had hoped; I am going to revise my work and ask for help from my teacher.
I've tried to learn my part for the musical, but I just can't get it. I knew I shouldn't have tried out. I'm not talented enough to be on stage.	I am struggling to learn my part for the musical. I think I should try a different strategy, such as creating an audio recording so I can listen to my part rather than just read it.
During my mile run, I came in last. I'm not an athlete and I'll never meet my personal goal.	I came in last on my mile run today, but I didn't have to walk and I shaved 2 minutes off of my personal best.

Now tell students to think of a personal fixed-mindset trigger. Encourage the students to anonymously write their fixed-mindset trigger on a notecard. Once all the notecards have been collected, shuffle the stack and redistribute the cards to the class. Put students in partner groups or triads and instruct them to brainstorm strategies for addressing the fixed-mindset triggers indicated on the cards. Ask students to view the trigger through a growth-mindset lens and write suggestions on each notecard to address the fixed mindset.

Prompt group discussion by asking students to identify what people who have a fixed mindset focus on and how they respond to new learning, challenges, mistakes, effort, and struggles.

Review the ideas and strategies generated by the students and allow them an opportunity to collect their own cards and reflect on the peer responses. Reflective practices encourage the development of deeper learning and connection. Encourage students to think about what they will do when they encounter their fixed-mindset trigger.

Reflective practices include:

- Journaling or blogging about ways to work through fixed self-talk.

- Identifying connections and/or *aha* moments through conversations with peers.

- Drawing or sketching their mindsets.

- Designing a comic strip story to illustrate steps for changing mindset.

CHECK FOR UNDERSTANDING

- Check student reflections to determine if they have made connections regarding how outcomes can vary depending on whether the situation is approached with a fixed or growth mindset.

- Extend the lesson by helping students identify goals, potential obstacles, and action steps for practicing growth-mindset strategies when they encounter a fixed trigger.

MORE THAN PRAISE

In an interview with *The Atlantic*,[18] Carol Dweck expressed concern that many teachers were misunderstanding growth mindset in a way that oversimplified the concept. Teachers, thinking they were practicing growth mindset, were praising student effort that resulted in no achievement (e.g., "Wow! You worked really hard on that test you just failed!"). In these cases, the praise became less about incremental progress and more about a "consolation prize," as Dweck puts it. She reminds teachers that growth mindset was developed largely as an antidote to the self-esteem movement, and growth-mindset praise should specifically focus on what progress came from student effort. If there was no progress, the conversation should be about re-strategizing.

There is so much more to growth mindset than just praising effort. If teachers hope to maximize the effectiveness of the mindset interventions, they must strive to present a growth mindset in the classroom every day and to be honest with themselves and their students when combatting a fixed mindset. To that end, we've developed a list of attributes of a growth-mindset teacher.

Equity vs. Equality	Understands the difference between equitability and equality, and works to provide learning opportunities and distribute resources in an equitable manner.
Action-oriented	Encourages students to solve their own problems; focuses on asking questions, teaching strategies, and offering support to promote problem solving among students.
Flexible	Understanding of different needs. Not rooted in harmful education practices like utilizing non-fluid ability groups.
High expectations	Has high expectations of every student. Models those expectations through body language, verbal communication, positive reinforcement, and constructive feedback.
Communicative	Offers lots of process-oriented feedback to students; students feel comfortable asking and answering questions.
Strong relationships	Demonstrates caring and concern for students; knows about students' lives, interests, passions, etc.
Process-oriented	Understands that learning is less about the outcome and more about the process. Praises and critiques the process, not the person.
Values mistakes	Normalizes mistakes and helps students value them as learning opportunities.

Empathetic	Makes an effort to connect and view challenges and struggles from a student's perspective.
Positive interdependence	Establishes a community of learners working simultaneously on personal learning outcomes and group goals.

A FIRM PLACE TO STAND

"Give me a firm place to stand, and I will move the Earth." The Greek mathematician Archimedes said that about his work with levers, but it can be interpreted another way, too. When students feel insecure or as if they don't belong or don't matter, they won't take risks, they won't step outside their comfort zones, and they won't make the kinds of learning achievements of which they are capable. An insecure environment is a breeding ground for fixed mindsets. The growth-mindset teacher gives students a firm place to stand by offering them a safe, secure, and supportive environment in which their growth mindsets can flourish, unbound by fear or judgment.

In the same manner, if teachers do not feel empowered to take risks in a safe and secure school community, they, too, will develop fixed mindsets. We know that a teacher with a growth mindset is one who can make a big impact in the lives of his or her students. We often use a quote from *Mindset* in professional development with teachers to drive home the fact that we cannot possibly predict the potential of our students:

> "...a person's true potential is unknown (and unknowable);...it's impossible to foresee what can be accomplished with years of passion, toil, and training."[19]

But that limitless potential does not only apply to students; it applies to teachers, as well. The ripple effect of our impact on students is unknown and unknowable. The habits and behaviors we help shape in our students now can have big consequences in their lives later on, both good and bad. We cannot precisely predict how what we do today will impact our students in the future. We cannot know what lesson, interaction, or piece of advice a student will carry with them for years to come. But research does tell us that teachers with a growth mindset can help their students develop resilience, hone problem-solving skills, and improve academic outcomes, so developing growth mindset in teachers seems to be an excellent place to begin in turning the sense of hopelessness that so many students feel into a sense of boundless possibility.

Here are some strategies you can immediately put into practice to start incorporating growth-mindset principles in your classroom:

- **Use process-praise in responding to student mistakes.** Give students specific feedback and critique on what they did wrong and ask them to identify strategies for improvement. Never make a failed assignment a referendum on student character—focus on the process, not the person!

- **Grade less, dialogue more.** Not every assignment needs a grade. Instead of putting a big red letter grade, percentage, or score at the top of every assignment, try handing it back with an insightful passage highlighted or piece of useful feedback instead. Get students used to the idea of working toward a learning goal, not a grade.

- **Highlight mistakes.** Create a bulletin board of "imperfect papers"— papers with great mistakes that illustrate an important learning process. Normalize mistakes by showing how student mistakes are part of the learning process; help them learn to deconstruct mistakes and then build on what works.

- **Read aloud.** Find an awesome children's book that demonstrates growth mindset (We like *The Dot*, *The Most Magnificent Mistake*, and *Rosie Revere, Engineer*, but there are many out there!) and read it to your students. Find other media (books, video clips, songs, poems, etc.) that demonstrate growth mindset, show them to your students, and discuss. (Check out our full list at the end of this chapter.)

- **Model growth-oriented self-talk.** Don't be afraid to share, share, share your errors with students. Talk out loud about your thinking processes. The more you model your growth mindset, the more likely your students will adopt it as part of their own self-talk.

- **Talk about the brain.** Some students need concrete evidence that this stuff really works. Dig into the neuroscience behind growth mindset. Conduct lessons and activities that teach students how their brains learn and grow. (More on that in Chapter 3, or check out the lesson plan for teaching students about how their brain learns in Chapter 3 of *The Growth Mindset Coach*.)

WRAP UP: YOU GOT THIS!

We know this chapter was kind of depressing. Kids have lost hope, they are reporting feeling uncertain and dispirited about their futures, and growth mindset is rendered ineffectual by fixed-mindset teachers. But there is good news: you. You are here, you are ready to learn, you want to get better, and that is what will make the difference. You can engage in practices every day to improve your growth mindset and help develop your students' mindsets. You don't have to do it in one day.

Remember the fable about the crow and the pitcher? A crow was dying of thirst and could find nothing to drink. The situation was dire. Finally, the crow came across a pitcher of water; her prayers were answered! But, when she peeked into the pitcher, there was only a bit of water left and the crow could not get her beak to the bottom to take a drink. So, she started dropping pebbles into the pitcher, one by one, until the water slowly started to rise. Eventually, the water was high enough so that the crow could take a drink of the cool water. Regardless of your circumstances, you can find ways to make small differences and improve the situation. It's never hopeless. Be the crow. Drop pebbles of empathy, understanding, compassion, and courage in your classroom every day, and watch your students rise to the occasion.

GROWTH MINDSET AND MOTIVATIONAL BOOKS TO EXPLORE

Making a Splash by Carol E. Reiley

Rosie Revere, Engineer by Andrea Beaty

Wonder by R.J. Palacio

The Dot by Peter H. Reynolds

Everyone Can Learn to Ride a Bicycle by Chris Raschka

Emmanuel's Dream by Laurie Ann Thompson

Drum Dream Girl: How One Girl's Courage Changed Music by Margarita Engle and Rafael López

Nadia: The Girl Who Couldn't Sit Still by Karlin Gray

Last to Finish: A Story About the Smartest Boy in Math Class (The Adventures of Everyday Geniuses) by Barbara Esham

The Most Magnificent Thing by Ashley Spires

Holes by Louis Sachar

Hatchet by Gary Paulsen

Sink or Swim by Valerie Coulman

Stuck by Oliver Jeffers

Fish in a Tree by Lynda Mullaly Hunt

Flight School by Lita Judge

2

PLAY 2: BUILDING POSITIVE RELATIONSHIPS

I've learned that people will forget what you said, people will forget what you did, but people will never forget how you made them feel.

—Maya Angelou

There is something truly, deeply, magnificently wonderful about every single student who walks through your classroom door. Sometimes we don't see it right away. Other times, it shines through like a beacon of potential. Many times we see it, but have a hard time convincing our students it is there. Part of our job is to draw that amazing, utterly unique specialness out of every single student—to help them see their limitless potential, their capacity for growth, and the power they hold within themselves to achieve incredible things. But here's the tricky part: It's impossible to convince a student of their own potential for greatness unless they have a reason to believe you. And students don't have any reason to believe you unless you have proven to them you're a trustworthy, credible source of information. Think about who you are more likely to believe: a near-stranger who barely knows anything about you except for your last assessment score, or someone who has put in the time and effort to know you, your history, and your interests? Forging deep and meaningful relationships is key to getting students to recognize their own potential. It's much easier to see something in yourself when someone else sees it in you, too. Maya Angelou's words are as true for students as they are with all people: Students will forget what you said, they will forget what you did, but they will never forget how you made them feel. So why not make them feel unstoppable?

LET'S SHAKE ON IT

In early 2017, a viral video made the rounds on the Internet. The video showed Barry White, Jr., a fifth-grade teacher from Charlotte, North Carolina, engaging in a special morning routine with his students. This unusual routine includes a complicated handshake with each one of his students. The children, lined up outside the classroom door at the beginning of the day, approach Mr. White and, one-by-one, engage him with a handshake of their own design.

It's truly a beautiful thing to see. From fist bumps to hand slaps to booty shakes to dabs to salutes, Mr. White makes his way through a series of choreographed handshakes with each of his students. You can see the enthusiasm heighten as the kids get closer to Mr. White—and closer to the entrance of their classroom.

"The most critical component is the relationship, the rapport you build with your students, because sometimes it can go underrated or overlooked," White told local Charlotte NBC affiliate WCNC. "Before I'm able to deliver a substantial amount of content to them, they have to invest in the teacher."[20]

Research supports White's belief that developing relationships is an important first step in learning. One study showed that early positive relationships with teachers were reflected by later academic achievement. Similarly, early negative teacher-student relationships were factors in predicting later negative outcomes. One study followed 179 students from kindergarten through eighth grade. Kindergarten teachers were asked to rate the quality of their relationships with students, as well as the students' overall behavior. Researchers tracked standardized test scores, grades, and discipline records of the students as they moved from first through eighth grade, and found that students whose teacher-student relationships were rated poorly in kindergarten had lower academic outcomes by eighth grade. But, if a student's behavior was rated poorly, those behaviors persisted. If the teacher-student relationship was rated highly, students were less likely to continue negative behavior patterns than the students with negative behaviors and low-quality teacher-student relationships.[21]

Educator Rita Pierson puts it best: "Every child deserves a champion, an adult who will never give up on them, who understands the power of connection, and insists they become the best they can be."[22]

When teachers take the advice of educators like White and Pierson, they set their students up for later success. But what about when those connections don't come so easy?

DEVELOPING RELATIONSHIPS WITH DIFFICULT STUDENTS

Shane was Laura's first, and perhaps most memorable, "difficult" student. He interrupted her in class, incessantly talked to others during instruction, and rarely finished his work. He was insulting, rude, and completely disinterested. Laura felt exasperated. Since day one, Shane had been difficult, she'd often fumed. He'd never even given her class a chance! Her anger with Shane was palpable. Anticipating his disruptions and disrespect, she'd snap at him, sit him away from the group, or tell him upfront—before he did anything wrong—that she was watching him and he'd better behave.

The more tactics to quell Shane's behaviors Laura tried, the more disruptive Shane became. One day, she complained about Shane to a group of teachers in the breakroom. One teacher seemed surprised at Shane's behavior. "He always works hard in my class," the teacher told Laura. "I'm surprised about how he's behaving for you."

Laura was stumped. She had assumed that all the teachers were having the same experience with Shane, and that they'd be ready to commiserate about his rotten attitude in class. But that wasn't the case at all. In fact, when she probed a little more about his behavior in other classes, she was met with confusion: His football coach complimented his work ethic at practice and the drama teacher said he was a leader in class. Then his math teacher said, "Maybe he's acting out because of his home situation? He's taking his parents' divorce pretty hard, so I've been trying to be extra compassionate."

What? She'd never even thought about his experiences outside of her class. The more she learned about Shane from other teachers, the more she realized the answer to her problem. Shane didn't show her respect because she hadn't earned it from him. The following Monday, she approached Shane and said, "Heard you had a great football game on Friday night. Way to go!" He thanked her and went to his seat. Later, during a lesson on Shakespeare, she said, "Shane, you're in drama, right? Which of Shakespeare's characters would you most like to play?" He seemed surprised by the question, but quickly launched into an answer. That day, Shane had zero behavior issues. Was it because his behavior had improved, or because Laura wasn't looking for problems?

Laura set an intention that week to not make any pre-judgments about how Shane might act in class and she resolved to make one personal comment to him each class period. Slowly but surely, her plan began to work. The more she got to know him, the more positive his learning attitude in class became. By the end of the year, Laura could honestly say that he was one of her favorite students. Did he talk out of turn sometimes? Sure. Could he be uncooperative? Occasionally. But she found that making efforts to know him on a personal level served to de-escalate situations with Shane. She also realized that his behaviors inside the class were a coping mechanism for something he was dealing with outside of class. Had she continued traveling down the vicious cycle of punishments, retribution, and blame, she was certain things would have gotten worse, not better.

IDEAS FOR BUILDING RELATIONSHIPS WITH STUDENTS

STRATEGY	WHAT IT LOOKS LIKE
Morning check-in	Have students sit in a circle and ask them to rate how their day is going so far. (5 = great, 4 = really good, 3 = fine, 2 = not so well, 1 = terrible). Pay attention to those students that give low ratings to the start of their day. Providing journaling time, drawing time, or one-on-one conferencing time will be helpful in moving them beyond any negative feelings they began the day with.

STRATEGY	WHAT IT LOOKS LIKE
"All About Me" bags	Students place three to five items in a bag that describe them. Students share the items and how each relates to them. Make notes on what the students share, and be intentional in creating personal interactions with each student that highlight the attributes and interests presented.
Agreements	Instead of a list of rules of what not to do, consider collaborating with students to develop a list of agreements needed to ensure the work you do together creates a growth-oriented environment. Developing the agreements helps you set the tone with students and highlights what you will foster in the collaborative classroom. (See Chapter 8 for more details.)
Q and A	Ask students questions and pay attention to their responses. This can be set up as a four corners task, where students answer the questions by moving to specified spots around the room, or they can answer questions by sharing answers with two other peers. Use student answers to help forge personal relationships.
Personalization	Students create personalized items (such as name tags, poems, songs, time capsules, inventories, or collages) to highlight their interests, likes, fears, hopes, etc. Appreciate differences! Understand how we all have limitations and strengths and how those characteristics make up the person we are.
Positive messages	Share a personalized positive message with a student or ask a question by writing it on a Post-It: How did the meet go last night? I really like how you handled the situation with the group work yesterday. How do you feel you did on the ACT? Great questioning in class yesterday! You really got us thinking!

A PERSONALIZED APPROACH TO PROBLEMATIC BEHAVIORS

An advantage of taking the time to develop positive relationships with your students is that when the time comes to have a difficult conversation or confront a behavior problem with the student, those talks will be more comfortable and, ultimately, more productive. Teacher-student relationships based on mutual respect and understanding can provide a firm foundation from which to springboard into these difficult talks. Teachers sometimes focus on negative behaviors that are disruptive to class, like constant talking, blurting, and interrupting behaviors. It is understandable to find these commonplace behaviors frustrating, because they can interfere with learning goals, but always focusing on negative behaviors may sabotage a teacher's ability to control them. Focusing instead on positive, meaningful relationships may help behavior management strategies be more well-received.

For this exercise, we'd like you to make a conscious effort over the next week to take note of the classroom behaviors that you witness. It may help to create a table to help collect your data, like this:

A behavior I observed...	A reflective question about this behavior...	A potential answer to my question...	An idea for seeking to resolve the issue I've identified...

For example, as you notice a behavior, jot it down in the first column under the heading "A behavior I observed...." It will also help if you record the date and time of the behavior in question. The more information, the better. Take time to reflect on how you might provide your student with the opportunity to control the behavior through questioning. You may ask questions to identify frustrations or consider ways you might change the environment to facilitate more desirable behavior (see second column). Then, use the final two columns to brainstorm potential solutions and results. Let's take a look at Johnny, for example. Here is an observed behavior:

- Johnny frequently interrupts the teacher in the middle of the lesson.

Instead of shutting Johnny down or punishing him in some manner, take a moment to ask questions about his behavior. Write these down in the second column.

- Why does Johnny interrupt me when I'm teaching a lesson?

- Is there something in the classroom environment I could change to encourage more appropriate behavior?

- Are there appropriate social skills that I could teach Johnny to help him grow in this regard?

In the third column, offer up some potential ways to answer your question. Setting up interventions that foster growth will likely lead to improvement in the behavior in question.

- Johnny lacks understanding about appropriate times to talk.

- Johnny lacks understanding about basic social skills.

- Johnny needs personalized supports to help him.

- Johnny is unfamiliar with the classroom rules.

- Johnny wants more control over his learning environment.

- Johnny lacks empathy for the people he interrupts.

- Johnny lacks the skills necessary for success.

In the final column, you'll come up with a solution that seeks to solve the problem and provide Johnny with an opportunity for growth. Instead of shutting Johnny down, approach him with empathy and seek to solve the problem in a collaborative manner, working together to develop strategies to help Johnny learn and demonstrate the desired behavior.

- Make a chart illustrating appropriate and inappropriate times to talk.

- Create a social story book, or other visual, that reinforces desired social behaviors.

- Use a hand-cuing signal to alert Johnny of times to talk.

- Review your classroom agreements with Johnny as often as necessary.

- Give Johnny more control over his learning environment. Providing him voice and choice may help him feel more secure.

- Give him an opportunity to lead the class, which may result in him developing empathy and gaining a better understanding of the importance of the act of listening.

- Give Johnny an opportunity to engage in self-reflection; try asking him to score himself on specific tasks, like how many times he interrupted, how well he listened, or how many questions he asked.

At the end of the exercise, you will have a clearer understanding of the issue and how best to proceed. Here's how the finished product might look:

A behavior I observed...	A reflective question about this behavior...	A potential answer to my question...	An idea for seeking to resolve the issue I've identified...
Johnny interrupts in class.	Why does Johnny consistently interrupt while I'm giving a lesson?	Johnny needs personalized supports to help him adhere to this classroom practice.	I will work with Johnny to develop personalized hand cues to let him know when he is interrupting and when it is an appropriate time to share his thought.
Sarah often falls asleep in class. (Monday at 9:15 AM; Tuesday at 8:20 AM; Friday at 9:05 AM)	Why does Sarah fall asleep in the middle of class time?	Sarah has been living with a noncustodial parent since being evicted from her primary residence. She also comes to school in the same clothes, which are often dirty, day after day. The instability in her living situation may be affecting her energy at school.	I will alert the counselor to my observations. Together, with any other necessary stakeholders, we will develop a plan for when Sarah falls asleep in class. I will also start a dialogue with Sarah to find out what, if any, of her basic needs are being met.

Taking time to map out a plan for success serves to clarify the situation for the teacher and give the student a clear picture of the issue and a path to improvement. When the situation is clearly defined, teachers can better identify potential causes of the behavior, and also discern where preconceived notions or judgments on their part may have colored the situation. Involving the student in collaborative problem solving will go further in helping to make a positive change than issuing top-down discipline, which often results in no positive change.

GET CURIOUS, NOT FURIOUS

Let's go back to Laura and Shane for a moment. Shane's behaviors in Laura's class were not just negatively impacting him; they were negatively impacting Laura, too. She was stewing over her relationship with Shane, and found herself doing things that she'd swore she would never do: talking badly about a student to other teachers, letting low expectations prejudice her against a student, and lashing out at a student.

Laura might have consciously or unconsciously been giving Shane signals that transmitted her disapproval and low expectations. Making efforts to develop relationships with students is easy at the beginning of the year when we don't know them yet. There is optimism in possibility. But what about when we're halfway through the year and we've been having the same trouble with the same student over and over again, and the relationship has become an extreme source of frustration? What then?

If you repeatedly find yourself at odds with the same student, try getting curious, not furious. There is little use in getting upset day after day about the same students' behaviors. If Laura had tried getting curious about Shane's behavior, instead of just being furious, she might have seen the situation improve much more quickly. If you're having difficulty developing a relationship with a student, start by asking yourself some frank questions about your attitude toward the student. Here's a reflective questioning exercise to try.

What are my honest feelings about this student?	
Am I projecting those feelings to the student during class?	

Do I give non-verbal cues that indicate my lack of expectation or care? (Eye-rolls, smirks, sighs, etc.)	
What situations most often trigger negative non-verbal communication?	
Am I expecting more out of my student than they can give at this time?	
Am I irritated by this student because I am otherwise frustrated, irritable, or in a bad place?	
Am I dwelling on negative behaviors with this student that I often forgive in others?	
What could I do to alleviate my frustration with this student?	
Have I considered all possible reasons for the behaviors the student displays in my class?	
What does my student enjoy? Am I making an effort to engage this student?	

Once you have an understanding of your feelings toward and responses to the student, you may be surprised to find that you are part of the problem, too. For example, if a student is constantly leaving in the middle of class to go to the bathroom, nurse, office, etc., consider that the student may be finding ways to leave class because they don't feel engaged. If students are constantly talking out of turn or among themselves during class, consider that you may not be giving them enough opportunities to speak during class time. Of course, there is an expectation that students abide by rules you have set in place for your classroom, but it is important that you fully assess whether or not those rules are realistic or necessary. Consider the following scenarios and decide how the student could make an improvement *and* how the teacher could make an improvement.

The situation	What can the student do differently?	What can the teacher do differently?
Ms. Franklin only accepts work done in blue or black ink. Ryan turns in a paper done in purple ink. Ms. Franklin gives the paper a 0.	Ryan could work harder to follow the rules.	Ms. Franklin could be more flexible and give students more choice. She could allow Ryan to turn in the assignment done in blue or black ink for full credit. She could reflect on the rule to determine its necessity.
Anna forgot her PE uniform. Her PE teacher, Mr. James, makes her run laps the entire class period as punishment.	Anna could put a system in place to help her remember her PE uniform.	Mr. James could keep spare PE uniforms or allow students to participate in street clothes in an effort to be more understanding that students can be forgetful sometimes. If forgetting becomes a problem, he could work with individual students on a plan to improve their accountability.
Tanner is caught copying homework from a friend in class. Ms. Gomez gives them both zeroes and a day of in-school suspension.	Tanner could ask the teacher for guidance, ask questions in class, attend a tutoring session, or try to grasp the concept or skill by viewing lessons online.	Ms. Gomez could provide formative checks in class to ensure students understand the lesson and homework. She could allow Tanner and his friend an opportunity to redo the assignment or demonstrate their learning by creating a video lesson. Ms. Gomez could also help Tanner and his friend learn more about the importance of peer coaching, as well as effective ways to guide one another.
When Zara talks out of turn, Ms. Timons takes away recess time. Zara has lost 5 minutes of every single recess this week.	Zara could write her thoughts on a sticky note to be shared at more appropriate times.	Ms. Timons could create predictable times for Zara to share her thoughts or provide opportunities for her students to connect to their learning by conversing with their peers. Ms. Timons could help Zara establish goals to improve behavior. She may refer to the classroom agreements or share specific strategies that Zara might use. Ms. Timons may also consider giving Zara a set number of "passes" for talking out and reducing those "passes" as she demonstrates success using the strategies. Praising Zara on using talk-times effectively will also be an important step in helping Zara understand appropriate times for talking in class.

When we seek to find ways to connect with students, especially those who can trigger our fixed mindsets, we are doing ourselves a favor, too. But difficult behaviors aren't the only hurdle when it comes to developing high-quality relationships with our students. Sometimes the pressure to stick to the curriculum and the lack of time available to work on relationship-building can rob us of opportunities to get to know our students, and according to research, that's bad for teachers, too.

POOR TEACHER-STUDENT RELATIONSHIPS AFFECT TEACHERS, TOO

In an article about teacher turnover rates on theconversation.com, teachers intimated that they often felt so rushed and pressured at school to focus on the curriculum, they didn't have time to develop meaningful relationships with students. One teacher recalled a time she took a visibly distraught student in the hallway during class time to find out what was wrong. The student revealed that she had just found out she was pregnant, and was upset. During the hallway chat, the teacher's administrator walked by and saw her talking to the student in the hallway and later gave her counseling for failing to keep her other students busy.[23]

Research has also indicated that while negative teacher-student interactions can be a significant source of stress at work for educators, positive relationships with students act in the opposite manner, serving as a buffer against occupational stress.[24] So what can we do when pressure to stick to rigid schedules and routines prevents us from devoting necessary time to building relationships with students? Here are some ideas:

Dialogue journals	Embed relationship-building in your curriculum with dialogue journals. This is a way for students and teachers to keep a running dialogue through writing. It develops students writing skills, but also helps build relationships.

Socratic Seminars	Use the Socratic Seminar method to get equitable participation in class discussions. Often, just a few students dominate our class discussions. When we set up opportunities for all students to speak, we can have meaningful interactions with students who sometimes don't get attention during class.
2×10 strategy	The 2×10 strategy is simple: Spend 2 minutes per day for 10 days talking with a student. Meet them before school as they eat breakfast, after school as they wait for the bus, or during recess, lunch, or transition times, etc. Talk to the student about his or her interests (favorite food, what he/she did over the weekend, a hobby, an extracurricular activity, etc.)
Attend events	See your students in action outside of school. Head to the soccer fields, check out a local play or musical, or volunteer to help with events that your students will likely be attending.
Stand at the door	This tried-and-true method of standing at the door to greet your students can set the tone for the day. Go the extra mile to notice and mention things about your students: what they are wearing, a new haircut, small talk about last night's game, etc.

The more efforts you make to talk to your students, about their work or otherwise, the stronger your relationships will become. Remember, building relationships with students is a win-win situation: It makes school a happier and more satisfying experience for both students and teachers.

WRAP UP: THE STAR THROWER

At a conference recently, we heard Claire, a secondary teacher, say, "I work with over 100 students every single day. I cannot possibly have a relationship with each one of them." To that, we say, give it a shot. You might not find success in forming deep and meaningful relationships with every single student, but in your efforts to achieve it, you will make a difference to many. If you're ever feeling overwhelmed or like what you're doing isn't making a difference, just remember this story:

> A man walked along a beach thinking to himself. Far ahead, he saw someone moving in a peculiar manner. He rushed to catch up, curious as to what this person was doing, moving in such an odd manner down the beach. He realized, as he caught up to his fellow beach dweller, that it was a man throwing starfish into the sea. "What are you doing?" he demanded,

to which the starfish thrower replied that he was throwing the starfish into the ocean because the tide was going out and they would die otherwise. "Don't you realize," said the man, "that there are many miles of beach filled with many thousands of starfish and you cannot possibly work fast enough to make a difference?" The young man picked up a starfish, chucked it into the ocean, and said, "I made a difference to that one."

Do what you can with what you have and continue to seek out ways to do more. It's the growth-mindset way and will produce better results than not having tried at all.

3

PLAY 3: BRAIN TRAINING

The capacity to learn is a gift; the ability to learn is
a skill; the willingness to learn is a choice.

—Brian Herbert

We get it. Trying to convince some students of their potential can be nearly impossible. Maybe they've been labeled a "bad kid" by other teachers, maybe they've had a family member tell them they were stupid or hopeless, or maybe their fixed mindset has prevented them from believing that they are capable of achieving great things. Whatever the reason, these tough customers often won't accept the mindset argument at face value—they want proof. Luckily, they've got three pounds of proof right inside their skulls. Yep, we're talking about the brain. Neuroscientists have definitively concluded that the brain is a malleable organ, and that with dedication and focused practice, it is capable of some truly incredible things. If a person can believe that muscles can get bigger through lifting weights, then they can believe that the brain can get bigger—and smarter—through study and hard work. The human brain is a complex and wondrous thing, and helping your students understand exactly how the components of the brain are engaged in the learning process will help them buy into the idea that their brain, like everyone else's, has the ability to grow and change. Once kids understand the power they have to grow their own brains, being "smart" becomes less an abstract quality that only some people possess and more an outcome that can be achieved by anyone willing to work for it.

THE BRAIN IS LIKE A MUSCLE THAT GROWS

In our first book, we talked in depth about how the brain is similar to a muscle, in that with dedication and training it can strengthen over time. Much of the science behind growth mindset is rooted in the idea that, like plastic, the human brain is malleable. *Brain plasticity* is the term neuroscientists have given to the ability of the brain to continue to change over time.[25]

There are about 100 billion neurons in the human brain. These little cells store information and send and receive messages all over our bodies. When we learn something new, our neurons send signals to each other through neural pathways to carry out the task. The more you work on the task, the faster the signals move through the pathway. If you stop doing the task for a prolonged period, the neurons will move more slowly. Imagine you're walking through the forest. At first, as you walk through the woods, it's hard to get anywhere. You have to move brush and navigate around obstacles, all the while getting thwacked by branches—it's slow going! But the more you walk the path, moving the brush, avoiding the obstacles, and trimming the branches, it becomes much easier to navigate. Eventually, you create a well-worn path in the earth, quite easy to walk down. The same goes with developing neural pathways. The more we practice a skill, the quicker our neurons fire. Scientists like to say, "neurons that fire together, wire together."[26] As the neuronal path gets used, it becomes easier for neurons to travel, and things that were once slow-going become well-worn skills.

So, let's say our students are learning long division. They will utilize their schema (things they already know) along with new information to complete the task. At first, they will work slowly to complete long division problems as the neurons fire slowly and begin to chart their course. As the student practices the skill of long division over and over, the neurons involved in the process will begin to travel the pathway more quickly. Suddenly, long division becomes less of a struggle and more of a skill.

For many years, scientists believed the brain was most malleable in childhood, but they have recently discovered the brain retains its malleability our entire lives. We can learn new skills well into old age. The more we work on a task, the better our brain becomes at carrying out the function. You know the old adage "practice makes perfect"? It's not just a meaningless platitude. Think back to the path for a moment—what if you stopped walking the path for several months? Likely, it would begin to grow over. Similarly, if a student stops doing long division for an extended period of time and tries to pick it back up, he or she will likely struggle a bit. This is the neurons reacquainting themselves with the task. Another cliché, "use it or lose it," applies here as well, as neural pathways that stop being used begin to degenerate.

These adaptive capabilities underpin the theory of growth mindset. It is possible to learn new things and strengthen neural connections throughout our lives. This is why we, as teachers, just cannot accept it when students argue they are "not a math person" or "not athletic." Sure, some people are born with a seemingly natural affinity for things—singing, reading, sports—but ask anyone who has risen to the top of their field and they will tell you, regardless of the starting point, it takes hard work and training to become highly skilled at any given pursuit.

OUR CHANGING BRAINS
MINI-LESSON

LEARNING OBJECTIVE

At the end of the lesson, students will be able to:

- define brain plasticity

- understand how it plays a role in learning

RESOURCES AND MATERIALS

- Paper

- Pencil

METHOD

Note: You may first want to teach the lesson on parts of the brain from Chapter 4 of *The Growth Mindset Coach* before introducing this lesson.

First, ask students to get out a piece of paper and write their name at the top. When the students are finished writing their names, ask them to write it again, but this time using their non-dominant hand. Now, ask them to wad up the piece of paper and throw it. Then, ask them to pick up the paper and do it again with the non-dominant hand.

Continue asking them to do tasks with their dominant and non-dominant hands. (e.g., blow your nose with a tissue, write on the board, open a locker, open your book, etc. This is a good chance to get the students up and moving.)

After the students have had the opportunity to experiment with using their dominant and non-dominant hands, have them record how they felt when they attempted a task using their non-dominant hand using sticky notes (one word per sticky note) or an electronic word cloud generator. (See example on next page.)

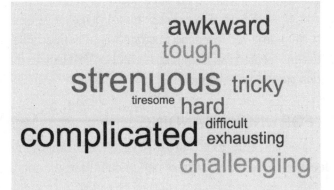

awkward
tough
strenuous tricky
tiresome hard
complicated difficult
exhausting
challenging

Put all the words together in one place and ask students: Is there a time you've experienced these feelings when you're learning something new? (Prompt students to share a time they felt frustrated, challenged, etc., at school). Now ask: What do you think would happen if you could only use your non-dominant hand from now on? (Possible student response: "You'd get better at using it.")

Say: Right! You would improve over time! This ability for the brain to change, make new connections, and learn new things is called brain plasticity. Right now, doing things with your non-dominant hand feels [insert some of the feelings students reported], but if you were to keep at it, it would become easier because your brain would get used to doing it that way. People used to think the brain couldn't change much. But scientists have learned that our brains are changing all the time. When you work hard on something or practice really hard, you get better at it. Can you think of something that you weren't very good at doing, but then got better? (Possible student responses: spelling, riding a bike, playing soccer, etc.)

Say: That's right. With hard work and effort, we can train our brains to get better at doing anything, including things at school like math, science, and reading. Remember how we talked about "growth mindset"—believing that with hard work and effort, you can improve at anything? Well, our brains are what makes that true! When we start working on a new skill or sport or concept in school, our brains get to work right away, making connections and figuring out the new thing we're doing. The next time we work on something new in class, like a math concept or a difficult spelling word or a science experiment, and it feels [insert feelings that students reported during exercise], just remember that is your brain at work. We're going to keep this list of feelings posted in the classroom. Next time you're feeling frustrated or uncomfortable [again, refer to student-created list] then just remember, that feeling means your brain is growing and changing.

CHECK FOR UNDERSTANDING

Continue to reinforce the idea that learning new concepts sometimes evokes feelings of discomfort. Check periodically that students associate that discomfort with learning by taking moments of frustration in class and asking students to explain how that frustration and struggle are signs that their brains are growing. Remind them about brain plasticity, if necessary. (Keep the word cloud posted in the room as a reminder, too!)

PRACTICE WITH PURPOSE

"You know what they say, Mom," Marc proudly told his mother, "Practice makes—"

"Perfect. I know the saying," Marc's mother interrupted.

"No, mom, that's not how my teacher taught me," said Marc. "My teacher says, 'practice makes permanent.'"

Brain plasticity—the ability of the brain to change over time—is an important concept to teach your students. Not only does it underpin the mindset theory, but the clear-cut scientific research may help buoy the acceptance of growth-mindset skeptics. But, beyond teaching our students how their brains work, we must teach them specific practices and methods to optimize learning. One such theory into optimal learning, as young Marc pointed out to his mother, is that practice makes permanent.

In the book *Make It Stick: The Science of Successful Learning,* Peter Brown and his coauthors, psychologists Mark McDaniel and Henry Roediger, tell us that we must practice how we want to play, because we will play like we practice. They illustrate this point with an anecdote from the Minneapolis Police Department:

> The Minneapolis Police Department conducted an officer training exercise in which two officers would practice disarming a perpetrator. The officers play act the parts of the cop and the perp, and, when the gun is pointed at the officer, the officer would use a move to break the wrist and take the weapon. In the exercise, he'd hand the gun back to his practice partner and continue practicing the move over and over. But, in this case, the officers weren't practicing like they wanted to play. Because when the time came to employ the move in the field, one officer who was able to successfully pull off the wrist-break maneuver then handed the confiscated weapon back to the criminal, just like he'd done in practice so many times before! Luckily, the officer and the perp were so confused by what had happened, the officer managed to get the gun back, but it was clear: The training needed to change, because the officer's brain played like it had practiced.[27]

Growth mindset isn't just about working hard, it's about working hard and smart. The police officer in the story likely practiced that move a hundred times, but he wasn't practicing it in a way that helped his brain make sense of the task in a variety of situations. We cannot just expect our students to get better by reading more or reviewing the study guide longer; we have to offer useful tips and strategies proven to aid in learning. If students don't know how they best learn, no amount of studying is going to make the information stick. Fortunately, lots of research has been done into how the brain best learns new information. Let's examine some evidence-based strategies that optimize learning. For students, using these strategies will help build stronger, longer-lasting neural pathways.

STRATEGIES FOR SUPPORTING NEW LEARNING

STRATEGY	DESCRIPTION
Quick quiz	Set aside three to five minutes to allow for a low-stakes quiz so students can practice retrieving newly and previously learned information. (More about retrieval practice on the next page.) Provide quizzes that allow for recall, not just recognition. Avoid using the quizzes as a tool for grading; rather, provide effective feedback and use this opportunity to help students learn and retain the material.
Distributed practice	Allow for practice to be distributed. Consider spreading practice opportunities over the course of several days by offering a few problems each day, rather than one large practice exercise on a single day. This helps students get into the habit of working the skill over time.
Productive struggle	Offering challenging tasks that require students to use critical-thinking skills and apply effort will lead to better retention. Provide opportunities for students to engage in rigorous learning. Remember, some struggling helps train the brain to learn and retrieve information.
3-2-1	Have students write down three things they learned from a previous class period or today's learning, two things they found interesting, and one question they have about the content.
Entry ticket	Connect the learning from a previous day, engage students in new learning, or make the learning relevant by connecting it to a concept in students' lives by inviting them to answer an open-ended question prompt, solve a problem, identify a misconception, or ask a question. Provide a structured and routine time for students to think and share their thoughts.

Technology	Use technology (such as Clickers, Poll Everywhere, Padlet, and NearPod) or labeled index cards to provide opportunities for students to retrieve and work through their learning. Ask questions or survey students to gather insight on their learning and processing of information. Pose questions that can be coupled with flash chats (quick partner talks) as a chance to explain thinking patterns, rationale, or as a time to ask peer questions.
Formative checks	Question responses can be recorded on whiteboards or slates. (Make your own dry erase form by inserting copy paper into a page protector.) Have students record their answers and show their work. Facilitate around the room to check for understanding and provide effective feedback.

RETRIEVAL PRACTICE

Research has shown there are proven techniques for study and practice that dramatically increase the odds of information retention. We must teach our students that not all study methods are created equal, and help them see that studying in a calculated way will increase outcomes. Of course, what works for one student may not work for another, so it is important that students experiment with study methods to find what is successful for them. (We'll talk more about personal learning styles in the next chapter on metacognition.) One such type of study method is called retrieval practice.

Pooja Agarwal is a professor, cognitive scientist, and founder of the website retrievalpractice.org.[28] On the website, Agarwal details why many of the study methods students use today don't serve them well, and how they can change their study habits to better retain information.

Teachers, Agarwal contends, are usually focused on getting information *into* student brains through the delivery of content, but often don't consider how the student will get the information *out* later on. Agarwal says that despite their popularity, classic methods students typically employ to retain information for future use, like rereading a chapter, going over notes, or highlighting important passages are not very effective. These short-term methods may help students as they dive into an all-night cram session for tomorrow's midterm, but the "crammed" information won't stick in their brains very long. People in the fixed-mindset zone are often focused on performance, so if cramming nets an A on the final, then it feels like a success. But when operating in the growth mindset, where learning is the outcome, one quickly realizes that crammed information rarely lasts longer than the following day and ultimately doesn't serve the mission of deep, authentic learning.

Instead of focusing on short-term learning, Agarwal says that we should focus on long-term learning through retrieval practice. What is retrieval practice? Put simply, it's the practice of retrieving information from our minds. Instead of attempting to jam more information in through reading, lecturing, and going over notes, retrieval practice is the slow (and sometimes painful!) process of forcing our brains to recall information. Quizzing is an example of retrieval practice. When you teach a lesson and give a quiz on it the next day, you are asking students to pull out of their minds what you put in them yesterday. But what if you quizzed them again a week later? Two weeks? Three weeks? Would they remember?

Continuous efforts to pull information from the brain is central to retrieval practice, and, as Agarwal and her colleagues believe, the secret to long-term learning. Their research revealed that among students who used retrieval practice as part of their study, 67 percent reported feeling less test anxiety.[29] To take advantage of retrieval practice as a learning strategy instead of an assessment strategy, it's important to incorporate it in meaningful, non-punitive ways each day.

We've created retrieval practice prompts for exit and entry tickets as an example for how retrieval practice can be used in the classroom. Remember, for retrieval practice to be most successful, it should be part of the learning routine, met with useful feedback, and used as a low-stakes method for reinforcing learning.

Two things I remember from yesterday's lesson are:

1. _____

2. _____

Two things I remember from today's lesson are:

1. _____

2. _____

If I could ask my teacher to explain something in more detail about today's lesson, it would be...

If I had to explain _____ from yesterday's lesson to someone who missed class, here's what I would say:

Help the teacher write a question for a quiz on today's learning:

Draw a picture that represents what we learned today.

Yesterday's lesson made me think of:

WRAP UP: THE BRAIN GAME

Hey, why don't you write down three things you learned in this chapter?

1. _____

2. _____

3. _____

How did you do with retrieving the information? See what we did there? Seriously, this chapter is all about teaching students how their brains are capable of major growth, and how to optimize that growth for success. Teaching the science behind mindset is a non-negotiable part of developing a growth-oriented classroom. Neuroplasticity may seem like a difficult concept for kids to understand, but it's actually pretty simple: When we work hard and practice, our brains grow and develop. Once students understand that, they can speak the language of mindset more fluently. A mistake is just the brain attempting to make new connections. Frustration is a feeling associated with the brain mapping out a new neural pathway. And, of course, learning something new feels weird, like using the wrong hand to write your name, because your brain is doing something it's never done before! Once kids begin to understand how their amazing brains work, they will be less likely to view struggle and challenge as personal faults and more likely to see them as parts of the process of learning. When they reach that point, you can ramp it up by teaching them how to engage in intentional, focused practice to make the most of their learning.

4

PLAY 4: MISSION: METACOGNITION

Knowing others is intelligence;
Knowing yourself is true wisdom.
Mastering others is strength;
Mastering yourself is true power.

—Laozi

A common complaint we hear among teachers is that their students are incapable of solving problems. But guess what? Very rarely have these teachers actually attempted to solve their own problem of having a lack of problem solvers. Listen, we totally get what you're saying. It's no secret we're living in the age of helicopter parents and instant gratification. We're not questioning whether or not the problem-solving issues exist; we're asking, what are you going to do about it? This chapter is all about helping students become masters of their thinking. If we want to develop problem solvers, we have to stop offering up all the answers. Letting kids struggle in a productive way is a good thing. If you want problem solvers, stop swooping in and taking over, and start forcing students to plan, strategize, and evaluate in an intentional way. Huddle up! We're diving into metacognition, what it means to teach students how to think about their thinking, and how letting students wrestle with their problems is the answer to your prayers.

MORE THAN THINKING ABOUT THINKING

From a very young age, human beings begin using metacognitive strategies as part of their learning process. Metacognition is often defined as "thinking about thinking," though that is somewhat an oversimplification. It can be better described as understanding and having control over the higher-order thinking processes associated with learning, such as planning, strategizing, and evaluating progress. Metacognition is a conscious approach to thinking and learning; when students are able to view their thinking and learning as a process of implementing strategies and evaluating outcomes, they can apply that learning to a variety of situations far beyond the immediate context in which they are working. For the metacognitive student, learning becomes less about the outcomes of learning (*I got an A on the test!*) and more about the process of learning (*X strategy contributed to my success on the test*).

Metacognition is a critical process of growth mindset. If we tell our students that their brains have the ability to grow with practice and hard work, we also must give them the tools that maximize that growth. Last chapter, we talked about specific strategies like retrieval practice that can help optimize learning. Strategies like these can be utilized in the practice of metacognition. Teaching our students about metacognition, and how people must be intentional in the way they plan, strategize, and evaluate their learning, helps develop independent learners who are able to take specific strategies that work for them and apply them to any number of applicable learning scenarios.

Teaching metacognition is important for a number of reasons, not the least of which is that it develops useful habits for later in life. If we ask students to complete a task in school, for example, but do not also ask them about the learning and thinking that helped them achieve the task, the experience will be simply isolated to achieving the task. When we encourage students to monitor and reflect on their own thinking, we help them see how completing the task involved skills and strategies that can be useful on a number of other tasks as well. This reflection and awareness of precisely what actions and strategies helped students in achieving an outcome contributes to developing useful learning habits their whole lives long.

HOW I LEARN BEST

In their book *How Did You Get Here? Students with Disabilities and Their Journeys to Harvard*, Harvard professors Thomas Hehir and Laura Schifter recount how students who make impressive academic achievements, like attending Harvard, despite a learning disability that may have otherwise hampered their success, have something in common: They are excellent self-advocates. They truly understand the limitations their disability creates and develop a repertoire of strategies and techniques for overcoming or circumventing those limitations. Understanding exactly what you need to be successful in any learning scenario is not just useful for students grappling with disability; understanding how you learn best and being able to articulate that is useful for any student.[30]

Education consultants Bena Kallick and Allison Zmuda write in their book *Students at the Center*: "From the outset of every task, it is important for students to think about their thinking—considering their work habits, reflecting on their capacity to persist, and remembering the strategies that have worked for them in the past."[31] Indeed, having a solid understanding of what work habits promote effective learning and what strategies have aided success in the past are critical components to practicing effective metacognition.

Often, we don't take time to think about the strategies we depend on as learners to get the job done, but articulating them can help develop a methodology for optimal learning. Whether or not you've taken the time to write them down, there are probably some go-to strategies that you have developed that help you find success in learning. Think about strategies you use to plan for, monitor, and evaluate after learning. Here are some that we notice in our own learning.

- Annie is an auditory learner. She retains information better when she hears it out loud, and often stops during silent reading to read important passages out loud so she can better understand them. She often questions herself aloud while reading, to stay on top of comprehension. When her comprehension wanes, she rereads and tries a different strategy, like annotating the confusing passage to make meaning in chunks.

- Annie gets easily distracted in noisy environments. She does best working in silence, but when that isn't possible, she finds playing classical music through noise canceling headphones is helpful in helping her achieve focus.

- Annie sometimes has difficulty re-thinking her initial strategies. She tends to formulate a plan and continue on with it, even if it stops working. Because she understands this propensity toward stubbornness, she makes a point to stop frequently and ask herself questions like: Is this strategy working for me? Is there another way I could accomplish this more effectively?

- Annie struggles with attention span. If she is studying or learning a new task and feels herself getting frustrated or notices that her mind (or Internet browser) is wandering, she gets up and takes a walk or otherwise separates herself from the learning, and comes back to it when she's prepared to focus.

- Heather is a visual and kinesthetic learner and often takes notes to connect and outline her learning. She responds to retaining information by rewriting or constructing her learning in manageable chunks or in a way that allows her to "do" the work in some way, shape, or form.

- Heather finds it necessary to have an orderly learning environment free of clutter, messes, disorganization, and distractions. She finds or creates a space that is tidy, clean, and free of unnecessary stuff.

- Heather uses goal-setting or creates "to do" lists to help her work through large tasks. Marking items off the list or celebrating small successes toward meeting a larger goal helps her stay focused and committed to completing the job.

- Heather seeks to share her learning and involve others in the process. Gathering the feedback and insight from those around her helps her to better construct and retain the information in a more meaningful way.

Now, take a moment to think of strategies you use in planning, monitoring, and evaluating your learning.

1. _____

2. _____

3. _____

4. _____

5. _____

6. _____

METACOGNITION: AN EXPLAINER

If metacognition is largely self-awareness about our needs as learners, then helping students develop metacognitive strategies must begin with helping them articulate how they learn best. Having students identify the metacognitive strategies that help them learn best can serve you as the teacher, too. When you know the conditions under which your students do their best work, you can differentiate and personalize instruction and provide supports that create optimal conditions for your students. Start by surveying your students on their current metacognitive strategies. Students might not be familiar with the word "metacognition," so begin by explaining what you mean by metacognition.

One way to explain metacognition to students is to liken it to learning a new skill. Let's use "how to hit a baseball" as an example. When first attempting to hit the baseball, a batter will test out different strategies in an attempt to find what works best. The batter will adjust her stance, crouch lower or higher, move toward the plate or away from it, alter her grip, raise or lower her bat, and so on, until she find the stance that works for her. It might take some frustration and failure in the form of strikeouts and other challenges before the batter gets it right. Once the batter finds a batting method that works for her, she sticks with it, but with the understanding that it is important for her to continually check in with her stance, because a change in environment (e.g., a left-handed pitcher vs. a right-handed pitcher, etc.) may prompt her to make a small adjustment.

Like the batter, students should consider a number of factors and test out strategies to discover what works best. Unfortunately, many students do not do this. Many with a fixed mindset assume they are genetically predisposed to being bad learners, but that is likely because they haven't come up with the right strategy yet. Often, if the first strategy they try or the most traditional strategy does not work, they chalk it up to being slow learners or not cut out for school, when, more likely, they haven't stuck with it long enough to find the strategy that works for them. Assuming one is bad at learning before making efforts to find what works would be like a batter walking up to the plate and hacking away at the air without making an effort to learn how to bat. Just as the coach's job is to help a player develop into a successful batter, our job as teachers is to help our students develop into successful learners.

CREATING THINKING JOURNALS
MINI-LESSON

LEARNING OBJECTIVE

At the end of the lesson, students will be able to:

- understand the definition of metacognition

- assess their own metacognitive practices using the self-assessment tool

- create a Thinking Journal for use throughout the year

RESOURCES

- A notebook for each student

- Writing utensil

- Metacognition self-assessment

METHOD

First, introduce the vocabulary word "metacognition." Tell students that metacognition is when we use our brains to think about how we learn best. Metacognition is used in planning out, monitoring, strategizing for, and evaluating the outcomes of learning. Use the baseball analogy from before to describe metacognition, or devise one that resonates with your students. Next, deliver a Metacognitive Survey to students. (Note: You can select just a few of these questions or rewrite them in a way that serves your students.)

METACOGNITIVE SURVEY

- Describe a time you felt frustrated learning something new.

- What do you do when you don't understand something?

- How do you connect new information to things you already know?

- Describe the feeling of learning something new.

- What felt confusing about what you learned today?

- Did you have any challenges in today's learning? How did you overcome those challenges?

- What could you have done better to improve your learning today?

Ask students to pair up and share answers to the questions on the survey. Then, have them share their answers with the group. Make a master list of the student answers. Sometimes students don't realize that people experience learning in different ways. Some students may have similar responses, while others might diverge completely. Make a point to celebrate both the similarities and differences in learning, continually reminding students that all people learn differently.

Next, ask students to pull out the notebooks they will use for their Thinking Journals. (Variation: Students can use their regular journals in which to complete thinking exercises throughout the year.) Explain to students they will be keeping a Thinking Journal. This journal is designed to keep track of their thinking processes, strengths, and weaknesses as a learner, strategies that aid in learning, and reflection on learning experiences. Explain to students this is useful in developing their metacognitive skills.

For the first assignment, review the definition of metacognition and ask students to create a thinking self-portrait, featuring descriptions of themselves as learners. They can use their responses on the Metacognitive Survey to guide them, if necessary. Or, you could come up with one and share yours as an example. Here's an example of a student's thinking self-portrait:

Ask students to share their thinking self-portraits in pairs.

CHECK FOR UNDERSTANDING

Review journal entries to check student understanding of metacognition. Ask students to create a new self-portrait at the end of the year as a reflection on how their metacognitive practices have developed over time.

MORE ON THINKING JOURNALS

Thinking journals are excellent tools for getting students to think about their thinking. Use prompts like, "How were you successful today in class?" Or, simply encourage students to write about the thoughts and feelings they experienced during learning. Some guided journaling is helpful, especially those activities that focus students on dissecting their thinking during the three main parts of learning: planning, strategizing/monitoring, and evaluating. Here are more examples of journal entries.

In this example, Sarah's teacher has asked her to create a chart featuring her metacognitive approach to planning, monitoring, and evaluating. This gets Sarah thinking about the things that help and hinder her as she tries to learn material in class. Writing down these processes will help Sarah reflect on them more easily, and remember them next time she's engaged in learning.

Sarah's Metacognitive APPROACH!!!

Planning

- I can ask myself how our old lessons will connect to this new one?
- I'll prepare myself for best learning— avoid distractions & turn off phone!
- I will set a goal that will help me!

Monitoring

- I will annotate my textbook article to make note of connections or questions.
- I will skim the text FIRST and figure out where the most important parts are.

do this in the planning stage, too!!

Evaluating

- I will write a list of ?s I have
- I will make flash cards and quiz myself on important points.
- I will use our class thinking stems of think out loud w/ a partner.

I ♥ F.C. (I love Flash Cards!)

Here's another example, in which Sarah's teacher has asked her to complete thinking stems about a novel the class is reading. The thinking stems prompt Sarah to consider how the reading connects to things she already knows or has experienced in her own life. Doing this type of writing reflection work can result in interesting insights a student may not have arrived at otherwise.

My Thinking Stems

I'm thinking... To kill a Mockingbird reminds me of the stuff we learned about Jim Crow in history class.

This reminds me... of my favorite books as a kid because a young kid is narrating the story. This has some tough issues for a kid to be dealing with (like rape and racism), but it seems less scary through the eyes of a kid.

I'm connecting this story... to my own life. Jem & Scout judged Boo Radley, but they were so wrong. It makes me reflect about times I have been judged wrongly and how that felt, which makes me wonder about how people have felt when I have wrongly judged them.

Prepare some sample thinking stems to help get students thinking about the planning, monitoring, or evaluation on their thinking. Keep them posted in the classroom for use in journaling, to prompt discussion, or to serve as sentence starters when students are sharing aloud in class.

- I know I'm learning when…

- I'm picturing…

- I'm wondering…

- This reminds me of…

- I'm thinking…

- I'm noticing…

- I'm feeling…

- I'm curious if…

- I'm connecting this to…

Consider using the Thinking Journal as a standalone journal, or in combination with another journal the students keep in class. Make sure to offer feedback on the journals to continue the dialogue about thinking and promote further analysis and introspection.

MORE METACOGNITIVE STRATEGIES

Now that students have identified how they best learn, help them employ those strategies, explore new strategies, and update their repertoire of meta-cognitive tools. It's important to name these strategies and explain how they are used in thinking. As teachers, we often use these tools without naming them or identifying their purpose, but it's important that students explicitly understand these activities have a name and purpose so they can articulate how the strategies aid in their learning.

Activate prior knowledge	Begin new tasks by activating prior knowledge. Help students connect new learning with old thinking. Showing them which strategies they have used in the past will be helpful in this new learning scenario.
Check in on learning	Encourage students to articulate metacognitive strategies as they work through the process of learning. A running dialogue about strategies that are useful or detrimental to thinking and learning will help them associate specific strategies with success.
Use metaphors to help students understand metacognition	"Driving your brain" is an excellent example we've heard. Tell students they are the drivers of their brains, and like drivers on the road, they need to employ specific strategies to help them get to their destination. They may need to stop and ask for directions, take a different route, etc.[32]

Understanding strengths and weaknesses	When students are aware of the things they are already good at and those areas in which they struggle, they can use that information to their advantage. Help students identify their strengths as learners, and how they can use them as an antidote to their learning limitations.
Self-assessment	There are many self-assessment tools available. Use these to give students many chances to check in on their own thinking.
Peer assessment	Sometimes we miss things about our own thinking or lack the framework necessary to employ strategies that might make all the difference. Creating an environment in which peers can offer one another feedback in a non-judgmental way can make a big difference in your students' success with metacognition. A teacher that values metacognition is one who positions students to be both teachers and learners of metacognitive practice.
Feedback	Feedback is critical in developing metacognition. Without it, students may continue on the wrong path, using strategies that are not serving them. By asking questions, offering advice, and providing feedback, teachers can help students more deeply examine their metacognitive practices.

WRAP UP: DEVELOPING PROBLEM SOLVERS

As we said at the beginning of this chapter, we often hear teachers bemoaning the fact that today's kids just aren't problem solvers, but many of those same teachers do not make an effort to explicitly teach and practice problem-solving skills. Teaching students about metacognition and providing regular practice can address this issue by providing a framework for problem solving. In a classroom that acknowledges the critical role of metacognitive learning, teachers use questioning and verbal prompts to help students solve their own problems. Here are some questions you can use to help students stretch their problem-solving muscles.

- Can you define the problem that you are trying to solve?

- What strategies might you use to solve this problem?

- What outcome would you like to see?

- Can you think of some steps to arrive at that outcome?

- If your first attempt at solving the problem didn't work, what obstacles prevented you from solving the problem?

- What changes could you make to improve the outcome?

- How can you use this experience to solve other problems in the future?

- You know what the problem is, now what are you going to do about it?

In many cases, you must encourage students to be problem solvers. Often, they aren't solving their own problems because they don't have to—there is always an adult nearby willing to do it for them. Instead of just giving students the answer or guiding them to it when they cannot come up with it on their own, encourage them to engage in metacognitive strategies. This kind of thinking has all sorts of applicability in school and life. By promoting metacognition in your class, you will be promoting self-efficacy, problem solving, and critical thinking among your students.

5

PLAY 5: AFTER THE FALL (FAILURE AS A PATH TO SUCCESS)

The greatest glory in living lies not in never falling, but in rising every time we fall.

——Ralph Waldo Emerson

One of the pervasive myths about creativity is that the most brilliant ideas and inventions come from flashes of great inspiration or genius—the lightbulb moment, so to speak. But even the lightbulb, according to Thomas Edison, required 10,000 prototypes before he nailed it. Big results require hard work. Yep, plain ol' hard work; you know, that thing your dad kept railing on about on Saturday mornings as he tried to get you out of bed to rake the leaves. All the greats agree that while sometimes flashes of inspiration strike and result in magnificent outcomes, the key to success is arduous, disciplined, old-fashioned work ethic. It is the people who show up, plod along, and put the work in day after day who produce, achieve, and succeed. But those people are not without failure. In fact, it is often through acts of struggle, failure, and resilience that they arrive at their greatest discoveries. Remember that lightbulb? Edison didn't get discouraged at his 10,000 failures; in fact, he didn't even look at them as failures: "I have not failed. Not once. I've discovered ten thousand ways that don't work," Edison famously said." In learning, as in lightbulbs, success doesn't come easy. If your students aren't struggling, they very likely aren't learning up to their potential. Embedding productive struggle and positive responses to failure in your classroom practice means that when it's game time for students—taking a big test, giving a speech, learning a new skill, trying out for the school musical—they won't crumple under the weight of struggle and failure; they'll use it as a springboard to success.

POKE THE BEAST

In our presentations to faculties on growth mindset, we attempt to engage teachers in a quick exercise that will give them the sensation of struggle. We ask them to draw a sketch of their favorite animal to share with the group. Here are some of the responses we hear muttered in conversation as teachers work on their sketch:

- "I hate drawing."

- "I stink at drawing."

- "I didn't know there would be drawing."

- "My favorite animal is bear, but I drew a fish because I know how to do that."

- "Wow! Nancy drew a perfect koala bear. I can't compete with that."

- "Of course the art teacher's is going to be amazing."

- "I'm the art teacher and I feel so much pressure to be amazing."

- "I don't want to share my work."

- "Tell me what to draw."

- "What's the point of this?"

- "I really don't care about getting better at art."

We also see non-verbal cues of discomfort:

- Rolling eyes

- Wide-eyed disbelief

- Sighing

- Defeated posture

- Attempts to cheat or trace

- Uncomfortable laughter

Most people aren't confident in their drawing skills, so conducting this exercise all but guarantees a few fixed mindsets will be triggered. For teachers, who spend their professional lives being the expert in the room, struggling can be a foreign sensation. Yes, it's true, teachers. We see you and we know your secret: You hate to struggle just like students do!

Our fixed mindsets are most likely to come out when we get out of our comfort zones. If you don't know what operating in the fixed mindset feels like, then it will be much harder to help your students navigate it. So poke the beast! Try to learn how to play piano, dust off your old calculus books, make a complicated recipe, or learn to solve a Rubik's cube. Try something that will be challenging so that you can immerse yourself in struggle. When your fixed mindset starts to rear its ugly head, practice ways to overcome it with a growth-mindset voice. This exercise can help you empathize with struggling students dealing with their own fixed-mindset beasts.

PLANNING TO FAIL

The phrase "struggling student" has become a pejorative in some schools, but if students don't encounter struggle at school, are they even learning? If we wholly embrace the concept that growth is in the process, not the product, then we must acknowledge struggle as a key part of the process. Learning is not linear. It is jagged, imperfect, and messy. Normalizing struggle and failure in the classroom is the mark of a growth-mindset teacher. What do we mean by "normalize" struggle and failure? Let's look at some key steps:

- Explicitly teach students that struggle and failure are valuable parts of the learning process.

- Develop a plan students can use when encountering struggle and failure.

- Teach students about perseverance and resilience and offer opportunities to demonstrate them in learning.

For a long time, surviving hardship and struggle was the American Way; from plucky settlers standing up to the monarchy to forge a new democracy, to early pioneers making long and dangerous journeys West to find a better life, to women and minorities tirelessly fighting violence and oppression to seek equal treatment in the eyes of the law. While there are still many struggles for equality and fairness taking place every day, relentless hardship isn't as much of an inevitable consequence of living in America as it was once. In fact, many parents try to shield their children from any kind of heartache or disappointment in a misguided attempt to protect them. Because many kids don't have opportunities to develop character traits like grit, resilience, and perseverance as a natural part of life, it's prudent we make an effort to help develop them in our classrooms.

ACKNOWLEDGE THE INEVITABILITY OF STRUGGLE

The first step in our plan to normalize struggle and failure in your classroom is to help students view them as key parts of the learning process. Many students, particularly those with a fixed mindset, approach learning with the belief that if they don't get it right away or if they frequently encounter struggle, they have some innate inability to learn the material. These are the moments you hear students proclaim: "I'm just not a math person!" "I'm just not a good reader!" "I'm just not creative!"

When those fixed mindsets are triggered, take time to reinforce the idea that struggle is a natural and expected part of learning. For example, share stories of how people who have achieved great successes experienced struggle and failure before arriving at those successes. This is an evidence-based approach to dealing with struggle in the classroom that has been shown to increase student achievement.[33]

In a study published by the American Psychological Association, researchers wondered if high school science students' responses to struggle might be influenced by an intervention that demonstrated even the most accomplished scientists encountered struggle.[34] Researchers divided students into three groups. In the first group, students read about the professional accomplishments of famed researchers Marie Curie, Albert Einstein, and Michael Faraday; the second group read about the personal struggles of the three scientists; and the third group read about intellectual struggles the three scientific giants encountered.[35] Here are examples for Albert Einstein.

Professional Accomplishments: Nobel prize winner who is still a household name; he is considered the father of modern physics.

Intellectual Struggles: Einstein was committed to revising his papers and ideas. When his theories were challenged, he viewed the criticism as useful feedback and used it to strengthen his arguments.

Life Struggles: Einstein's family moved often when he was a child. He dealt with struggles associated with being the "new kid," and often had to scramble to catch up with the learning pace of his new class.

In the stories that detailed the scientists' various life and professional struggles, there was also information on how they worked to overcome those obstacles.

"Many students don't realize that all successes require a long journey with many failures," said Xiaodong Lin-Siegler, PhD., the lead researcher on the study.

But giving students opportunities to see how famed scientists have experienced their share of struggle made a difference in their own science class outcomes. The 402 students included in the study saw an overall increase in science grades after the six-week intervention, with a notable increase for low-achieving students. However, among the students in the cohort who only read of the scientists' greatest accomplishments with no information on how they overcame struggle and failure, grades in science class actually went down.

Explicitly teaching students the value of failure in the learning process will help them connect to the figures they are reading about in their textbooks. If they can draw a connection between Einstein struggling to catch up with his class and some struggle or obstacle they are dealing with, they are more likely to see their own obstacle as temporary or something to be worked through, instead of a permanent dysfunction or failure. Use explicit teaching methods, like sharing stories of famous figures experiencing failure, along with informal exchanges to promote struggle and failure as normal and natural. This can be done by correcting fixed-mindset talk when you hear it. Here are some examples of what we mean:

REPHRASING FIXED-MINDSET TALK

WHAT THE STUDENT SAYS...	HOW YOU CAN REPHRASE IT...
"I suck at math."	"You haven't got it, yet, but you will. Let's take a look at what worked and what didn't with how you solved this problem.
"I am not a good writer."	"You are a writer-in-training. You think Shakespeare wrote *MacBeth* in high school? It takes practice to be great, so let's practice!"
"That was an idiotic mistake."	"Now that we've pinpointed where the mistake is, let's talk about ways to correct it."
"This is way harder for me than it is for other kids."	"You might not realize it, but every learner in this class struggles. Struggling just means you're learning."

PLANNING FOR FAILURE

Failure most often sends people spiraling into their fixed mindset when they have no plan in place to deal with it. But if students have a plan in place for dealing with obstacles and setbacks, they are more likely to stay in the growth-mindset zone and work through the issue. Developing simple If/Then plans for overcoming struggles is an excellent way to get students to see struggle as an inevitable part of the learning process. With the plan in place, the students have a path to getting back on course—or, at the very least, they'll have tools to build a path.

Here's how If/Then plans work. Instead of just setting a goal and going for it, students attempt to consider possible obstacles or setbacks they might encounter along the way. Then, they develop If/Then statements that identify the potential obstacle along with a positive response to it. Here's an example.

Goal: I will earn a solo in the spring choir showcase.

If/Then: If I do not earn a solo, then I will ask my teacher for ideas on improving.

If/Then: If I do not earn a solo, then I will ask for practice advice from students who did.

If/Then: If I do not earn a solo, then I will work hard at performing well in my designated part.

When big projects, tests, speeches, or other important events are on the horizon, take time to help students develop If/Then plans. Teachers can model this type of planning by engaging in it, too. In fact, If/Then planning for teachers is an excellent way to navigate the many difficult situations we find ourselves in each day.

If/Then Plan: If my students perform poorly on this test, I will review the data and reteach areas where they seem to be falling short.

If/Then Plan: If this student acts out in class today, then I will take a deep breath and stick to my behavior management plan.

If/Then Plan: If my request to attend this conference gets turned down, then I will find a webinar or streaming option, or try to connect with some of the presenters online.

For both the student and teacher, the act of engaging in If/Then Planning, or other types of planning for failure, helps us visualize many possible outcomes and solutions. If we aren't prepared when a failure comes, we quickly arrive at a variation of "I'm a failure," "I'm not good enough," or "I'm going to give up." When we have a plan in place, the next steps are a series of clear actions. When those actions are not pre-planned, many respond to failure not by figuring out the next steps, but by figuring out who's to blame.

In the fixed mindset, meeting a roadblock is seen as failure, and failure is the end of effort. The process looks something like this: Try, fail, give up. In the growth mindset, failure is a detour. The process looks something like this: Try, fail, try again, struggle, re-learn a skill, encounter an obstacle, seek help and advice, overcome the obstacle, succeed, continue learning. Make sure failure in your classroom is a detour, not a roadblock.

RISING UP

"We must always work, and a self-respecting artist must not fold his hands on the pretext that he is not in the mood. If we wait for the mood, without endeavoring to meet it half-way, we easily become indolent and apathetic. We must be patient, and believe that inspiration will come to those who can master their disinclination."[36]

These are words written in the letters of Pyotr Ilyich Tchaikovsky, Russian composer of famed ballets *The Nutcracker* and *Swan Lake*. Artists are often saddled with the stroke-of-genius myth, but Tchaikovsky is unequivocal: While inspiration sometimes shows up, just as often it doesn't. And if we wait until we are in the mood to work, we will rarely work at all. This ability to keep coming back to your work even when you don't feel like it, even when it's easier not to, even when you're convinced you have nothing left to give, is what we're talking about when we talk about perseverance.

Our final step in embracing struggle in your classroom is to teach students about resiliency and give them opportunities to demonstrate it. First, you must create the conditions in your classroom under which students have opportunities to demonstrate resiliency. This means you must give second chances. And third, and fourth, and fifth….We're not suggesting that you not hold students accountable for turning in assignments; we're simply saying that developing a culture where learning is never "done" can go a long way in developing grit and resiliency among your students.

Create a culture in which handing back a paper two or three times isn't out of the ordinary. The process of revisiting work, analyzing feedback, conferencing with peers, and trying again should be a common loop in your classroom. In a classroom that has truly embraced struggle and failure as powerful learning tools, the feedback loop is routine and not punitive. Grades are always in flux with the possibility of improving, and it is understood that true learning requires multiple attempts.

WHAT ADVICE WOULD I GIVE?

If students have a difficult time getting past a failure, try engaging in this exercise.

Katie has been struggling in Mr. Raymore's Spanish class. Despite having studied for what seemed like forever, Katie once again botched the latest quiz. She looked at her C- and burst into tears. Mr. Raymore took time to privately chat with her.

Mr. Raymore: Katie, I can see you're upset at your grade. What's the problem?

Kate: I studied so hard for this! I just stink at Spanish. I'm going to drop the class.

Mr. Raymore: Katie, what grades did you get on your last two quizzes?

Katie: An F and a D.

Mr. Raymore: Let me ask you, who's your best friend?

Katie: Sheree.

Mr. Raymore: Okay, if Sheree was sitting here crying and told you the same thing you just told me, that she's going to drop out of the class because she got an F, D, and C as her three latest quiz scores, what would you tell her?

Katie: I don't know.

Mr. Raymore: Would you tell her she stinks at Spanish and she should drop the class?

Katie: No, I wouldn't tell her that! That's mean!

Mr. Raymore: Then why are you telling yourself that?

Katie: I guess I see your point.

Mr. Raymore: What would you tell Sheree if she were feeling how you are right now?

Katie: Well, I would tell her that it seems like her quiz scores are getting better every week, and she should just keep sticking with it.

Mr. Raymore: Anything else?

Katie: Maybe that she could ask you for some help, or another student who does well in class, if she feels like she needs to.

Mr. Raymore: So, do you think you can try to give yourself the same grace and encouragement that you would give to Sheree?

Katie: Yeah, I think I can do that.

When someone's fixed mindset takes over, moving the situation into the hypothetical realm for a moment can help them think more clearly about their response to failure. Try reframing the same situation, but as if a best friend or sibling were experiencing it. Often, we show forgiveness to and encourage resilience in others, but don't extend the same grace to ourselves. In this case, Katie felt like a failure for getting another below-average grade on a Spanish quiz. But when Mr. Raymore reframed her negative self-talk as advice to her friend, she was horrified.

WRAP-UP: KINTSUGI

In Japan, the art of Kintsugi, or "golden joinery," is a method of mending broken ceramics that dates back over 500 years.[37] When a ceramic is broken, instead of throwing it out, Japanese artisans repair the broken pieces with a golden lacquer, resulting in a ceramic object with a web of lovely gold veins running through it. These restorations are not seen as a flaw in the piece, but as part of its history and something that makes it uniquely beautiful, and more interesting and valuable than before.

Likewise, experiencing struggle and failure does not lessen our value as human beings. If we let them, those experiences of struggle and failure can ultimately add to the value of our lives by teaching us that though we may break on occasion, if we have the courage and resilience to repair ourselves, we can come out more beautiful and valuable than before.

6

PLAY 6: THE SHAME GAME

Shame corrodes the very part of us that
believes we are capable of change.

—Brené Brown

Brandon had a junior high football coach who always managed to make him feel like garbage. If this coach's assessment of Brandon was true, he was slow, lazy, stupid, and didn't even have the work ethic God gave a sloth. In short, this particular coach's philosophy was motivation through shame. Many adults—teachers, coaches, and even parents—are under the mistaken assumption that shame can act as a motivator. But the truth is, all shaming students does is belittle kids and make them feel unworthy and unloved. Was Brandon great at junior high football? Not particularly. Could he have been great? We'll never know. Because midway through the season, he got fed up and quit. In this way, shame breeds fixed mindsets: Tell kids they stink often enough, and pretty soon, they'll start to believe you. In this chapter, we're going to take a look at shame. What is it? How can we limit it in our classrooms? How can we manage its effects? Those people are right: Shame is a powerful motivator. Just not in the way they think. It motivates people to shut down, withdraw, and disengage.

Most often shame is employed in times of discipline, but if we were to ask any teacher to define discipline, we doubt any would answer that it's "a tool used to make children feel bad about themselves." No, they would tell us discipline is about providing guidance and helping students make better choices. Let's figure out how to move beyond the shame game and discover strategies for helping our learners make better choices.

THE EVOLUTION OF PUBLIC SHAMING

Miranda Larkin was the new kid at Oakleaf High School in Clay County, Florida. On her third day at her new school, a teacher informed her that her skirt was too short; the Oakleaf High School handbook said skirts and dresses can be no more than 3 inches above the knee. Miranda's was 4 inches. Miranda was sent to the nurse's office and given an oversized bright yellow shirt with the words "DRESS CODE VIOLATION" emblazoned on the front in large, black letters.

School officials defended the practice of making dress code violators wear the embarrassing shirt, and Larkin's mother filed a lawsuit against the school. In an interview with the *Washington Post*,[38] Dianna Larkin said she believes that there must be consequences when rules are broken, and that her problem was not with the dress code. "My problem," she said, "is with the public shaming of kids."

Public shaming has come a long way since the days of the dunce cap. Parents shaming their kids publicly, in particular, has become part of the Internet's cultural zeitgeist. Google "parent shaming" and you'll see pictures of kids holding poster board–sized neon signs proclaiming things like "I am a bully. Honk if you hate bullies," or "I lie. I steal. I sell drugs. I don't follow the law," and under the images you'll see a slew of anonymous comments complimenting the child-shaming parent on a job well done. One viral video that depicted a father shooting up a daughter's laptop in retribution for her insubordination has garnered over 40 million hits on YouTube. We're getting the sense that society is becoming indifferent to shame. Many of us disapprove of these big glaring acts of public shame, but beyond those, there are millions of little insidious acts of shame that happen in schools every day.

WHAT IS SHAME?

When we talk about shame, we're talking about a myriad of experiences. Here's a common shame scenario: You see an acquaintance across a crowded room meet your gaze with a wide smile and enthusiastic wave, but when you return the smile and wave, you realize it was meant for a person standing behind you. Ouch. That hurts. In that moment, you experience a sinking feeling in your stomach and would love nothing more than to turn tail and run. You might think to yourself, *I'm such an idiot!* This is shame, although in its most fleeting form—momentary embarrassment. It's something we all feel; a common sensation while navigating the human experience. Shame and vulnerability researcher Brené Brown describes shame as "the intensely painful feeling or experience of believing we are flawed and therefore unworthy of love and belonging."[39]

When we feel self-conscious in a crowd, we are experiencing a form of shame. When we feel like losers for failing to meet an objective, we are experiencing shame. When we suffer persistent feelings of inadequacy, mediocrity, or unworthiness in our professional or personal lives, this is shame. Shame is a powerful emotion, because while we are in the process of experiencing it, we feel unworthy and unlovable.

Brown, who has studied shame extensively, wrote on her blog: "Based on my work, I do believe that shame is still one of the most popular classroom management tools," and went on to say that in conversations with research subjects on the topic of shame, 85 percent of the people interviewed said they remembered an instance from school where they felt so ashamed, it changed the way they thought of themselves as learners.[40]

A shame-free classroom, of course, is an impossibility. Just as you cannot control whether all your students have a growth mindset, you cannot prevent them from experiencing shame in your classroom. Something as fleeting as an eye-roll or a snub from a classmate, often undetected by you, the teacher, has the potential to make a learner feel shame.

Shame and growth mindset, of course, are inextricably linked. They are two sides of the same coin. Schools intentionally and unintentionally contribute to the culture of shame, like when failure evokes feelings of inferiority in students, when students are publicly condemned as "bad" by having to pull a red card or write their name on the board, or when they are treated as pariahs forced to wear their failure like a big, yellow T-shirt, they are experiencing shame. And a school that embraces a culture of shame is not one that can embrace growth mindset as a path to achievement.

The cornerstone of growth mindset is the individual belief that our qualities, traits, and abilities are not fixed in nature, but that with dedicated practice, hard work, and effort, we can achieve in all areas. When enough people in your school embrace this ethos and share it with others, a pro-growth culture emerges. But in a culture that is ruled by fear and shaming, the growth mindset is subverted.

THE SHAME-AWARE CLASSROOM

Shame has deep implications for growth mindset. Growth mindset, at its core, is the belief that your traits and qualities can be developed over time. But, as Brené Brown said, "Shame corrodes the very part of us that believes we are capable of change." When we shame a student, we are also diminishing his or her capacity for growth.

What does a shame-aware classroom look like? For a long time, classroom management has employed tactics rooted in shame. In the shame-aware classroom, teachers avoid shaming students by developing more empathetic practices. First, we must be able to recognize the signs of shame. The easiest way to do this is to ask yourself what the inward and outward manifestations of shame look like for you. Perhaps your cheeks turn scarlet, you turn inward, you want to be alone, and you get very quiet and withdrawn. Think about a time that you have felt personal shame, and indicate what your self-talk sounded like during that experience.

When I feel shame...

I feel _____

I experience _____

I believe _____

I want _____

It's important not to only examine how you feel experiencing shame, but how you bounce back from a shaming experience. If you believe a student is experiencing shame, it is critical to talk about it. A classroom that can freely name shame and meet it with empathy, what Brown calls the "antidote" of shame, is a classroom that offers students a fighting chance against the destructive forces of shame. If shame is the feeling of unworthiness and being unloved, then when a student feels shame we must work to bolster his or her sense of value and belonging through words and actions. Where teachers and peers work to fight shame with empathy, shame cannot exist.

Here are some examples of classroom management practices that will help you limit shame in your classroom.

WHEN STUDENTS	DON'T...	INSTEAD, TRY TO...
Talk out of turn...	...write student's name on the board as a consequence.	...explicitly teach students when it is appropriate to talk and when it is necessary to listen. Create opportunities for sharing out loud daily.
Are caught texting...	...don't force them to read the text aloud.	...ask them to put the phone away, and later have a private conversation about the phone policy.
Perform poorly on a test or assignment...	...don't announce how many students failed.	...provide effective feedback and allow an opportunity for students who failed to redo the task.
Violate the dress code...	...don't send them home or force them to wear school-issued clothing.	...provide them with a copy of the dress code and offer concrete examples of what school-appropriate clothing looks like. If it must be addressed immediately, assist the student in discreetly calling a parent for a change of clothes.
Are mean to one another...	...don't call them bullies.	...hold them accountable for their behaviors, but continue to offer love and support.

QUITTING THE SHAME GAME IN CLASSROOM MANAGEMENT

Nikki Sabiston, a veteran elementary and early childhood education teacher in Virginia, made waves when she posted an article on her blog titled, "Why I Will Never Use a Behavior Chart Again."[41] Nikki's distaste for behavior charts started when her own son kept coming home from kindergarten feeling defeated because he never managed to stay green on his classroom behavior chart. She began to see the implications of behavior charts far beyond the classroom, including the psychological impacts that were manifesting in her own son.

"Kids do need reminders to stay on track. They do need consequences for negative behavior, and we should reward positive behavior," wrote Sabiston on her blog. "But not by causing stress, worry, and shame. I had to become a mommy and feel my own child's pain to see that."

She started to look at her own use of behavior charts through a more critical lens. She noticed that while the behavior charts tracked behaviors in her classroom, they did nothing to meaningfully change it. Many students felt the charts were a source of stress and were becoming demoralized, and the charts, by design, made the assumption that children were going to misbehave.

"They live in peril of either them or their friends having issues, or their friends getting moved down," said Sabiston. "You create this competitive mess that doesn't really help anyone behave better; it just creates fear, frustration, and anxiety."[42]

Instead of using behavior charts for classroom management, Sabiston made an effort to eliminate the shame-inducing behavior charts from her class and implement a classroom management system centered on communication and connection. She uses private conversations, verbal cues, and hand cues to offer students reminders of appropriate behaviors. Sabiston has a calming corner in her classroom where students voluntarily go so they can take a break and decompress. Sometimes she will ask a student to go there when they need to collect their thoughts for a moment, but she makes an effort to make it a happy space instead of a punitive one. There are even stuffed animals and stress balls to squeeze. When a behavior incident occurs, she focuses on getting curious, not furious. Her first step is just to ask the student to tell her the story of what happened.

"They are much more likely to be open and honest," said Sabiston. "In telling the story, they often come to the realization of what happened without my having to tell them."

Sabiston also makes a point to ask students how they are feeling, with the understanding that all feelings are okay. Once the student relays the story of what happened and describes how they are feeling, Sabiston next asks her student: "What should happen now?" She says rarely does she have to provide instructions for what the student should try to do to rectify the situation, because they usually come up with it on their own.

"If they don't come up with it themselves, then they won't learn," said Sabiston.

For teachers still using behavior charts, Sabiston says that while she understands the charts are a well-intentioned effort to keep students on track behavior-wise, there is a better way. She encourages teachers to try to look at behavior charts from the student's point of view, which she says can "remind us all to take a closer look at our little people from a different perspective."

BEHAVIOR MANAGEMENT BEYOND SHAME

It is possible to have a solid behavior management plan without invoking shame. Brown, in her widely-viewed TED Talk "Listening to Shame," draws the distinction between shame and guilt. According to Brown, guilt is "I did something bad," whereas shame is "I am bad."[43]

Let's look at this scenario:

David's teacher was having a rough day. The kids were acting out, a carefully planned lesson tanked, and she had some things going on at home. David was the straw that broke the camel's back. After speaking out of turn, his teacher scolded him, "Why can't you ever behave?" "I'm sorry," David replied, "I know I'm a bad kid." David's teacher softened and her toned changed. Had she implied that he was a bad person? She hadn't thought so, but clearly David had taken it that way. He could *never* behave, therefore, he was a bad kid. Yep, now she could see it.

Many teachers can empathize with David's teacher. Her sharp remark was a little too pointed. She was worn out, she didn't mean it that way. But the bottom line is, David took it that way. Instead of blaming David, she immediately started to repair the damage. She pulled David aside and offered an apology. She told him she cared for him and pointed out some of his finer qualities, and hoped that it was enough to make up for the damage her comment had done.

There are teachers among us, however, who deliver the sharp remarks without ever trying to repair the wound. David deserved it, they might say. If he hadn't spoken out of turn, they wouldn't have gotten after him, they'd say to justify their behavior. And, yes, that logic holds up for a moment, until you see that the teacher's language was imprecise. She evoked the feeling of shame (you are bad), instead of the feeling of guilt (you did a bad thing).

Ann Monroe, a professor of Elementary Education at the University of Mississippi, wrote in an article[44] published in *The Educational Forum* that while guilt and shame may appear to be similar at face value, research has revealed that the implications of the two emotions are very different.

"...more benevolent emotions, such as guilt and embarrassment, can serve the same regulatory function as shame without the potential for becoming an internalized, damaging force to our sense of self," writes Monroe. "Research has shown these emotions are less intense and carry far less destructive potential than shame."

We're not suggesting that teachers and schools should not enforce disciplinary practices when a student breaks a rule. But the language of and approach to discipline are incredibly important. The language must be precise. By saying, "Why can't you ever behave?" David's teacher made him feel unworthy, unloved, and bad. If she had pulled him aside and said, "David, please do not talk out of turn," David may have felt guilt for the infraction, but it would have taken him a far larger leap to arrive at "I am bad."

One consequence of frequently experiencing shame is disengagement. Brown says, "When we're disengaged we don't show up, we don't contribute, and we stop caring."[45] Let's look at the difference between a disengaged student and an engaged student:

DISENGAGED STUDENT	ENGAGED STUDENT
Withdrawn and doesn't speak in class, even when asked.	Answers and asks questions. Interacts with the material, teacher, and classmates.

DISENGAGED STUDENT	ENGAGED STUDENT
Hides face, sleeps, daydreams, or otherwise refuses to participate.	Listens attentively, offers ideas, collaborates with peers. Integrates themselves wholeheartedly in the coursework and among classmates.
Does not complete class assignments, homework, or otherwise does the bare minimum, performing far below potential.	Engages in work and puts forth clear effort and values learning opportunities.
Acts defensive, wearing proverbial armor to class as if they are going into battle.	Feels freedom to be vulnerable and takes educational risks; is not intimidated or fearful in the classroom.

It's important to understand what an engaged and a disengaged student look like, and also to acknowledge that shame can play a role in a student's withdrawing from class. If you notice that a student is disengaged, it may be because he or she is feeling shame. In this case, work to help the student overcome shame through offering empathy. (When a student is ready to engage, check Chapter 9 to explore strategies for increasing engagement.)

SCHOOL CULTURE AND CHANGE AGENTS

Writer and therapist Mary Pipher said, "Cultural change is a million acts of individual courage and kindness. That's the only way our culture has ever changed, and it's the only way it will change. And if you believe that, what that means is you're a change agent."[46]

Are you an agent for change in your school? In other words, are you contributing every day to the million little acts of kindness, or are you working against them? Remember Oakleaf High School, with the bright yellow shame shirt reserved for dress-code violators? Imagine if a small group of teachers refused to condone the practice of shaming students for too-short skirts are too-tight tops. What if they wrote letters, refused to punish dress-code infractions, and complained to administration about the practice? How long do you think it would continue to last?

Cultural anthropologist Margaret Mead is credited with the quote, "Never doubt that a small group of thoughtful, committed citizens can change the world; indeed, it's the only thing that ever has."[47]

Becoming a change agent in your school begins in your classroom. Schools experience all sorts of culture-level problems, from low staff morale and authoritarian administrators to lack of support networks for students. While these problems are often intangible, their effects are palpable. Toxic school environments, like those in which shaming students is part of the modus operandi of school discipline, can have devastating consequences for staff and students alike.

RECOGNIZING SHAME

The first step to shutting down shame in your school is to recognize it when it happens. Shaming happens despite good intentions. Classroom management tools like behavior charts, for example, are often taught in elementary education programs, so when teachers utilize those tools they may not realize they could be engaging in shaming practices. Likewise, in ability grouping, the goal is well intentioned: to work on reading instruction with peers at a similar reading level. But if there are lasting impacts on students' self-worth, we must ask ourselves if these types of potentially shame-inducing classroom practices are worth the short-term benefits. Let's take a look at some common shaming situations, and examine potential solutions that may lessen the amount of shame people experience at school.

SHAMING SITUATION	SOLUTION
A teacher has students pull a "red card" when they misbehave.	Make efforts to preserve student dignity by using one-on-one coaching or conferencing. Practice private conversations instead of public discipline.
A teacher makes a phone call home about a student's misbehavior in the presence of other students.	When discussing a student (even with other teachers), make sure the conversation stays private and professional.
Students are ability-grouped for reading instruction; all the students understand the "bluebirds" are the best readers and the "redbirds" are the worst.	If using ability grouping, make sure groups are fluid. When possible, mix up grouping practices to allow students to self-select, randomly group, or devise a variety of ways to group students.
A student caught texting in class is forced to read the text message aloud in front of her peers.	Remind the student of appropriate cell phone usage with private coaching or conferencing. If it continues to be a problem, develop a plan to implement logical consequences for the student in question.

SHAMING SITUATION	SOLUTION
An administrator engages in gossip about a staff member.	Instead of engaging in the gossip, respond with empathy, trying to reframe the situation through a lens of understanding.
You observe many fellow teachers have clear favorites among the students.	Make an effort to highlight positive aspects of all students—things they do well, areas of growth, etc.—particularly those students who may not be receiving positive feedback or reinforcement in other classes.
Staff members rarely accept accountability, and engage in finger-pointing and blaming behaviors.	Model accountability by making an effort to accept responsibility. Promote a culture of connection by demonstrating vulnerability, practicing empathy, and sharing useful information about high-functioning work groups.
A teacher routinely has students grade one another's papers or share grades aloud in class.	Always keep grade information private. Create a classroom culture that celebrates growth rather than traditionally "good" grades.

THE TALK OF SHAME

So how do you combat a shaming culture in your school? It's easy. When you see something, say something. Brown suggests that shame holds such power over people because it is rarely talked about. When we feel shamed, we want to crawl in a hole and pretend it never happened, not bring it up in conversation. Why share your humiliation? It would only prolong the feeling, right? Wrong. Brown says that shame's natural enemy is empathy. When we can talk about our shame to another person who expresses empathy for our pain, humiliation, or hurt, then it naturally lessens the shameful feelings. In other words, don't saddle up on your moral high horse and ride around your school shaming the shamers; that would be counterintuitive.

First, when a student comes to you expressing an experience of shame, don't shut them down. If a student, for example, says, "The gym teacher made me feel really stupid when I couldn't climb the rope today in PE," meet their shame with empathy. Say something like, "You know, when I was in elementary school, I could never get a handle on skipping, and all the kids made fun of me. It made me feel really bad, so I can imagine how you're feeling right now." Immediately, instead of experiencing the isolated feelings of shame and humiliation, the student now has a shared experience of empathy and belonging. You are a party of two who weren't perfect in gym class, and, yeah, it stinks, but it doesn't define you as a person.

Likewise, if you see a colleague shame a student, meeting that shame with equal parts shaming of his or her professionalism will only result in more people feeling bad. What can you do instead? Meet the shamer with empathy. Maybe it sounds something like this: "Man, I saw what happened with that student. I hate when that happens. I know it's really hard to handle situations like that. You know, I read a great article about dealing with students in those sticky situations. Would you like me to send it to you?"

Chances are the colleague who shamed the student was well-intentioned. They may have been trying to teach safety or respect, and it went awry. Very rarely is a teacher who shames a student doing it because they genuinely enjoy being mean-spirited. More likely, it was a tough situation that ended badly, and now they need empathy and compassion just as much as the student at the end of the shaming stick.

Let's take a look at some examples of shaming in school, and examine some potential responses.

SITUATION	DON'T	DO
A student complains to you that she felt embarrassed because a teacher sat her in a corner after she talked out of turn in class.	Don't march into the teacher's room and question her professional ethics.	Find a natural opportunity to talk to the other teacher about behavior management strategies you use with the students in your class.
A preschool student breaks all the crayons in a box.	Don't say, "You're so naughty."	Explain to the student the difference between a good choice and a bad choice. Explain that breaking all the crayons was a bad choice. Together, come up with ideas of what good choices look like.

SITUATION	DON'T	DO
You see a student make fun of another student for failing a test.	Don't yell at the student shaming a peer.	First, offer empathy and support to the student who failed the test, reinforcing the idea that failure is an opportunity for learning and growth, and remind the student of your confidence in their ability to build understanding. Secondly, ask the student shamer to engage in a perspective-taking exercise. Ask them how they would feel if someone treated them in the same manner. Ask them to reserve judgment of others until they make an effort to look at the situation from another perspective.
A former student has been removed from the classroom and is now sitting in the hallway, in the office, or in a buddy room.	Refrain from giving a look of disappointment, disgust, or frustration as you pass by the student.	Make eye contact and give an empathetic, genuine smile. Later that day or the next day, check in with the student and mention seeing them. Ask the student if they want to talk about what happened. If they do, engage in conversation that helps the student identify the problem and alternative solutions. If the student doesn't wish to discuss the situation, then leave them with the expectation that you know they will be able to do better next time. Make an effort to remind the student of their value and worth.

WRAP UP: MODEL, EMPATHIZE, CONNECT

We all feel moments of shame, even teachers. When you feel shame yourself or encounter someone else feeling shame, making an effort to reach out is the surest way to get on path the to healing.

"If we can share our story with someone who responds with empathy and understanding, shame can't survive," said Brown.

Developing a shame-aware classroom means having the courage to share your moments of shame with students and model that valuable, necessary step of reaching out and experiencing connection. Demonstrating empathy when students are feeling shame, modeling the value of human connection, and being courageous in sharing your own emotions will serve as a powerful example for students as they deal with shame in your classroom and beyond.

7

PLAY 7: THE HUMAN CONNECTION

Kind words can be short and easy to speak,
but their echoes are truly endless.

—Mother Teresa

Often, empathy is characterized by putting yourself in another person's shoes. Recent research has shown that the human brain is actually wired for empathy, but, as we know, if we don't strengthen those connections through regular practice, they get a little rusty. In this chapter, we're going to show you why empathy matters in the classroom. It can have implications in small moments, like when a student gets their feelings hurt at recess, but it also has larger ramifications. The often talked about school-to-prison pipeline is an example of how many of today's schools favor zero-tolerance discipline, which can lead to lifelong negative consequences for students, over practicing empathy and human connection in response to behavior issues. Ultimately, we want you to understand how practicing empathy every day, even in small ways, can strengthen connections with your students and then snowball into a host of other good things.

UNCONDITIONAL POSITIVE REGARD FOR TEACHERS

When we started writing this book, we felt we had to devote a chapter to growth mindset and its connection with empathy. Empathy, simply defined, is the ability to understand and identify with the feelings and emotions of others. Other people's lack of empathy—or the anticipated or perceived lack of empathy in others—is often the culprit behind fixed mindsets. People avoid trying new things or tackling difficult problems because they fear if they fail or struggle, others will judge them harshly. Think back to your own mindset triggers. You likely identified a scenario in which your fixed mindset manifests because of your fear that failure would make you lose value or worth in the eyes of another.

As we talked with educators, one school counselor mentioned that instead of using convoluted approaches to teaching empathy, she often shares with her colleagues and students an approach to relationships known as "unconditional positive regard." Rooted in the humanistic approach to psychotherapy developed by renowned psychologist Carl Rogers, unconditional positive regard has value in developing healthy and productive relationships at school and beyond. You may have read Rogers' popular work on person-centered teaching in your pre-service teacher training. Many of his therapist-patient relationship techniques have applicability in the classroom. Let's break down each part of unconditional positive regard: [48]

"Unconditional" simply means without conditions. In Rogers' own words, this "means that there are no conditions of acceptance, no feeling of 'I like you only if you are thus and so.'"

"Positive," in this case, means "prizing" of the other person, as Rogers wrote. Essentially, it is the acceptance of the person as a worthy, valuable, and whole being, which includes acceptance of both the "expression of negative" (i.e., unproductive feelings and behaviors) and the positive (i.e., productive feelings and behaviors).

"Regard" means to show respect to another person. It is holding another in esteem and viewing them as a capable person. As Rogers wrote concerning his therapy practice, "It means caring for the client as a separate person, with permission to have his own feelings, his own experiences."

So, how can we apply the unconditional positive regard approach at school? For teachers, it might look something like this:

1. I care about and want the best for my students regardless of who they are, where they come from, what I have heard about them, what they say, or what behaviors they display on a given day. My care and compassion is given freely without contingencies.

2. I will view my students as whole people. My students are more than the sum of their behaviors in my classroom. My students are unique, complex people worthy of love and respect.

3. In times of discipline and discord, I will continue to convey my respect and value for my students through my words and actions.

You can see how this approach to others has value to teachers and students alike. Teachers who want to demonstrate unconditional positive regard will avoid favoritism among students, treat all students with respect and dignity, avoid making students feel foolish, stupid, or shameful, and make an effort to develop meaningful relationships with all students.

UNCONDITIONAL POSITIVE REGARD FOR STUDENTS

To simplify the idea of unconditional positive regard so that our youngest students may understand, a teacher might create a set of class values that incorporate the tenets of unconditional positive regard. That might look something like this:

In this class we will…

- respect the choices of other people.

- recognize that all people have value and worth.

- strive to accept people without judging them.

- demonstrate compassion to other people.

Demonstrating unconditional value and respect for the humanity of students through your interactions and attitude can make for positive shifts in behavior, but it is not without controversy. Take Henry, for example. Henry was a kindergartner who demonstrated extremely aggressive behaviors. His teacher, Ms. Clinton, believed he was hurting underneath his tough facade. No matter what Henry did, Ms. Clinton never wavered in her commitment to acknowledge his value and humanity. He broke things, overturned desks, screamed expletives, refused to participate, and even hit Ms. Clinton on one occasion.

It wasn't that Ms. Clinton didn't deal with the issues; she made efforts to correct the behaviors every day through the use of logical consequences. But no matter what, when Henry walked through her classroom door, even if he was returning from being removed from the class, Ms. Clinton would reliably greet him with kindness and positivity. She made an effort to make Henry feel valued through her words and non-verbal cues like touch, eye contact, and smiling. Some teachers felt like showing Henry unconditional love and kindness was "going easy on him." But, Ms. Clinton believed that by the end of Henry's time in her class, showing Henry unconditional positive regard improved her relationship with him, improved the behaviors Henry exhibited in class, and stabilized his overall abilities to self-regulate and increase his feelings of self-worth.

Carl Rogers believed that children have two basic needs: positive regard and self-worth. Positive regard from others has implications for the self-worth of the child. Here is how Rogers viewed children with high self-worth and low self-worth:[49]

	LOW SELF-WORTH	HIGH SELF-WORTH
Confidence	A child with low self-worth lacks confidence and does not have positive feelings about his or herself.	A child with high self-worth has confidence and has positive feelings about his or herself.
Challenges	A child with low-self-worth avoids challenges, crumples under the stress of failure, and does not acknowledge or understand that life is inevitably unhappy at times.	A child with high self-worth faces challenges head on, learns from failure, and acknowledges that life is inevitably unhappy at times.

	LOW SELF-WORTH	HIGH SELF-WORTH
Other people	A child with low self-worth is guarded with other people. Often he or she will exhibit defensive or aggressive behaviors.	A child with high self-worth is open with other people, is open to criticism, and develops healthy relationships.

Ms. Clinton believed that Henry was struggling from low self-worth, and the best way to develop his self-worth was through unconditional positive regard. While others may have misunderstood Ms. Clinton's love and kindness for weakness and apathy, Ms. Clinton knew that in order to build Henry's self-worth, she must make him feel loved and valued at all times.

UNCONDITIONAL POSITIVE REGARD AND MINDSET

So how are unconditional positive regard and mindset connected? When a student understands they are loved, valued, and accepted because of who they are as a person, unconditional of their test performances, letter grades, or failures, they are more likely to develop a growth-mindset approach to school. Conversely, if they are valued as a student only when they perform well on a test or get an A on a paper, they will likely develop a fixed-mindset approach to school.

Many people think these two ideas—mindset and unconditional positive regard—are at odds with one another. Dweck, herself, has often stated that she developed the mindset theories as an antidote to the self-esteem movement. But treating people with esteem and falsely bolstering self-esteem are very different things. You can treat someone with respect while offering constructive criticism; the two are not mutually exclusive. Unconditional positive regard doesn't mean not helping students correct behaviors or never disciplining; it simply means that as you engage in helping change those negative behaviors, you maintain the focus on the action of the person, not on the nature of the person. There's a Swedish proverb that translates to "Love me when I least deserve it, because that's when I really need it." We must continue demonstrating care and concern regardless of the student behavior; conveying love and respect does not mean you are condoning the behavior, it means you are confirming their humanity.

SYMPATHY VS. EMPATHY

We learned in Chapter 6 that the antidote to shame is empathy. Developing empathy is non-negotiable for today's classroom teacher. We have no idea what our students may be experiencing at home—indeed, some of them may not even have a home—which is why it is critical they experience school as a place of love and belonging where they can leave their fears and worries at the door and fully engage in learning. We have to push beyond feeling for our students; we must feel with them. Feeling for our students is sympathy. Feeling with our students is empathy. It's easy to confuse sympathy and empathy, so let's take a look at a few examples.

Here's a scenario:

Kevin is an eighth grade student in Ms. Quinn's homeroom class. He also takes math with her. Kevin has been living in an apartment with his mother and grandmother since he was a baby. For the last year, Kevin's grandmother has been battling cancer. Kevin is absent for a few days, and Ms. Quinn finds out that Kevin's grandmother has died. When Kevin returns, he is sad and removed. Ms. Quinn pulls him aside to talk.

What Sympathy Looks Like	What Empathy Looks Like
Ms. Quinn: Kevin, I'm so sorry about your grandmother.	**Ms. Quinn:** Kevin, I felt so sad to hear about your grandmother's death.
Kevin: Thanks, Ms. Quinn.	**Kevin:** Thanks, Ms. Quinn.
Ms. Quinn: Are you doing okay today?	**Ms. Quinn:** Are you doing okay today?
Kevin: Yeah.	**Kevin:** Yeah.

Ms. Quinn: You know, your Grandma was a fighter. She fought that cancer all year. And I am so sorry, but at least now she won't have to live with the pain. And you'll have all those wonderful memories with her. **Kevin:** Yeah, I guess.	**Ms. Quinn:** Losing someone we love is so difficult and sad. I know you're hurting right now, and if you need someone to talk with, I'm here. I'll keep checking in with you. **Kevin:** Thanks, Ms. Quinn.

Do you see the difference? In the sympathy example, Ms. Quinn tries to put a positive spin on Kevin's situation. She tries to minimize his pain by "helping" him look on the bright side of his grandmother's death. In the empathy example, Ms. Quinn does not try to put a positive spin on Kevin's grandmother's death. Instead, she simply makes an effort to connect with him, let him know she understands the heartache involved in losing a loved one, and let him know she's available if he needs her. In the first conversation, Kevin will walk away and probably never approach Ms. Quinn about the subject again. She's feeling for Kevin, not with him. In the second example, Ms. Quinn acknowledges Kevin's pain, but makes no platitudes. She simply lets him know she understands what he is feeling and leaves the door open for more love and connection.

Let's look at another example.

Shanelle is a top student who is applying to several Ivy League schools. She has her heart set on Princeton, but is rejected. She gets into Cornell, but tells her teacher, Mr. Lee, that she's hurting over her rejection.

What Sympathy Looks Like	What Empathy Looks Like
Mr. Lee: Are you still upset about not getting into Princeton?	**Mr. Lee:** Are you still upset about not getting into Princeton?
Shanelle: Yes, I'm feeling really bad about it.	**Shanelle:** Yes, I'm feeling really bad about it.
Mr. Lee: That's a bummer, but you'll get over it eventually, I promise. And look on the bright side, Cornell is a great school!	**Mr. Lee:** I know what it feels like to really want something and not get it. That disappointment can hurt pretty bad. Do you want to talk about it?

In the sympathy example, Mr. Lee is attempting to show Shanelle kindness in her time of disappointment, but what he ultimately does is minimize her feelings. In the empathy example, Mr. Lee lets Shanelle know he knows how she is feeling, reserves judgment about her disappointment, and offers her an opportunity to connect. It's a small change, but sympathy, as Brené Brown says, "drives disconnection," while empathy "fuels connection."[50]

You can see how in the two sympathy examples, Kevin and Shanelle would most likely leave the conversations feeling like their teachers just didn't get it, while in the empathetic exchanges, they would leave the conversations feeling like someone might have an understanding of what they're going through.

Are you being empathetic or sympathetic to your students? Empathy is getting down in the muck and feeling with someone, without judgment. Sympathy is staring down at someone who's in the muck and offering unsolicited advice instead of love and support. Let's take a look at a few more situations that are common in schools and what they look like with a shaming response, a sympathetic response, and an empathetic response.

SITUATION	SHAMING RESPONSE	SYMPATHETIC RESPONSE	EMPATHETIC RESPONSE
A student fails a test they worked really hard to pass.	"You should have worked harder."	"At least it wasn't the final exam. If you work hard, you'll do better next time."	"It stinks to fail when we've worked so hard at something. Why don't we talk about what you can work on for next time?"
A student is disappointed they forgot to turn in a piece of homework.	"Hopefully you've learned your lesson about being irresponsible."	"I'm sorry you forgot to turn this in, but at least you'll know better next time."	"We all forgot to do things sometimes. Do you want to talk more about it?"
A student is teased by another student at recess, and reports the conflict.	"Don't be a crybaby."	"I'm sorry your feelings were hurt. Just play somewhere else and avoid that person."	"It hurts when others make fun of us. When you're ready, why don't we make a plan in case this happens again?"

SITUATION	SHAMING RESPONSE	SYMPATHETIC RESPONSE	EMPATHETIC RESPONSE
A student says he is feeling stupid after being enrolled in a remedial course.	"Work harder and you'll get to take classes with the regular kids."	"Don't worry. You're not stupid, you just need extra help. You'll be glad you did it."	"I know this feels bad. I had to retake a class in college once, and I remember feeling a lot like you are now. Do you want to talk about it?"

If you make an effort to change your words and practice empathy in small ways every day, your actions will become habits over time. You will transition from "doing" empathy in your classroom to being genuinely empathetic. Just as with growth mindset, we are all learners in this process. With intentional effort, empathetic behavior will become a matter of course, a new lens through which you see the world.

BUILDING EMPATHY
MINI-LESSON

LEARNING OBJECTIVE

At the end of the lesson, students will be able to:

- distinguish the difference between sympathy and empathy

- understand how to be an empathetic friend

RESOURCES AND MATERIALS

- Expression scale

- *Hey, Little Ant* by Phillip and Hannah Hoose

METHOD

SAY: Empathy means connecting with others and feeling what they feel without judging them. It is putting yourself in another person's shoes, and trying to see things from their point of view.

Share the expression scale above with students and explicitly help students identify how the facial expressions on the scale relate to feelings. Ask students to share with a partner a time when they could identify with one of the expressions and represented feelings. Share stories and model empathetic responses to their stories.

PLAY A GAME CALLED "WHAT'S MY FACE?"

Students stand in a circle and look at the floor. A student begins the game by thinking of an emotion and making a face to match the emotion. The first player will tap the person next to him or her on the shoulder. When the second player looks up at the first player, he or she will share the face. The second player will pass the expression on to the next player by tapping him or her on the shoulder and sharing the face. The expression is passed around the circle. Once everyone has had a chance to pass the face, the first player will say "What's My Face?" The players make the face and then share and discuss the feelings associated with it.

Read *Hey, Little Ant* by Phillip and Hannah Hoose. In the story, a boy attempts to squish an ant in an effort to impress his friends, but when the ant starts speaking to him, he learns a valuable lesson on empathy and perspective taking. During reading, stop and ask students to identify with the boy and the ant by naming and defining their feelings. Encourage the students to use the expression scale and share how the boy and ant might feel in the story. Ask students to write or draw an ending to the story that demonstrates what they have learned about empathy.

EXTENSION ACTIVITIES AND AGE VARIATIONS: Have students develop a class social story on empathy, or role-play what it looks like and sounds like to be empathetic. Take pictures of students acting out different situations and then have them write empathetic captions or a script. For example, students can pose in pictures that demonstrate a student has fallen and scraped his or her knee, has done poorly on an assignment, loses a toy at recess, has a friend move away, etc.

CHECK FOR UNDERSTANDING

Check student-created endings to *Hey, Little Ant* to see that they have demonstrated an understanding of empathy.

MORE BOOKS ON EMPATHY

Stand in My Shoes: Kids Learning About Empathy by Bob Sornson

The Invisible Boy by Trudy Ludwig

Red: A Crayon's Story by Michael Hall

Just Because by Amber Housey

Last Stop on Market Street by Matt de la Peña, illustrated by Christian Robinson

A Sick Day for Amos McGee by Philip C. Stead

Enemy Pie by Derek Munson

MORE WAYS TO MODEL EMPATHY TO STUDENTS

StoryCorps	Use the StoryCorps app and have students interview one another about their feelings, lives, experiences, etc.
Role-play	Describe a difficult situation to students, and have them act out an ending to the situation using empathy and kindness.
Socratic Seminar	Use techniques like Socratic Seminar to facilitate discussion of student thoughts and perspectives. Often, only a few students routinely speak up in class; this technique ensures all students are heard.
Media	Locate short films, songs, TED Talks, stories, or other media that share messages of empathy and kindness. Share them with students and facilitate a discussion or ask them to journal about how they made them feel.
Engineering project	When students identify a problem in society that impacts many people and develop a solution, they are engaging in empathy. Encourage students to design an engineering project that will result in good for the school or community. This is a great way to combine empathy study and STEM learning.

Empathy authors	Write a picture book about empathy for younger students. Have older students use difficult situations they have experienced, and show how kindness and empathy from another person helped them through it. Students can illustrate the book and read it to a book buddy.
Empathy Museum	Visit the website empathymuseum.com. Watch the short film on the various projects the Empathy Museum does to spread empathy on a large scale. Brainstorm ways to spread empathy in your school or community.
Humans of New York	Humans of New York (www.humansofnewyork.com) is a project that seeks to document the images and stories of people all over New York and the world. Share some school-appropriate examples from the Humans of New York project with students, and then ask them to photograph and collect stories from people in their communities. Storytelling is an excellent vehicle for discussing empathy and connection.
Other shoes: a perspective-taking exercise	Students choose a shoe from an assortment provided by the teacher and imagine the experiences of the person wearing the shoe. Students write or narrate a story from the perspective of the person they have created. They can share their work and determine similarities and differences among the shoe stories and reflect on how they can connect to people in different shoes.
Reflective practice	Introduce the proverb: "Don't judge a person until you walk a mile in their shoes." Ask students to explain in their own words what this means. Facilitate a discussion about this concept. Ask questions like: How does walking a few steps differ from walking a mile in someone else's shoes? How does the phrase "there are two sides to every story" relate to empathy? What other proverbs or phrases remind us of empathy practices?

Another empathy exercise to use in class is an empathy self-assessment. You can use these questions as journal prompts or checks for understanding for the lessons above. Use these questions to get students to explore their attitudes about empathy.

- Are you empathetic?

- How do you know when someone is being empathetic?

- What behaviors do empathetic people show?

- Describe, write, or draw ways to show empathy.

- What is the difference between sympathy and empathy?

- Why is empathy important?

Have students complete the empathy self-assessment by marking "Yes" or "No" to each of the following statements.

EMPATHY SELF-ASSESSMENT

	YES	NO
I think of the feelings of others.		
I often think of how I would feel if I were experiencing the situation.		
I often say the words, "Well, at least you…"		
I understand that everyone experiences things differently. I seek to understand others' perspectives.		
When I hear others share their story, I often want to help them feel better and move past the situation. I think of things to say to help them get over or through a situation.		
I seek to listen and feel what others are going through.		

Continue to make efforts to reinforce the value of empathy in personal relationships, the school community, and the wider culture. Model empathy every day and recognize acts of empathy that you see taking place at school.

RESTORATIVE JUSTICE

In any given school in America on any given day, there is likely a student who is absent because he or she has been suspended. Suspensions are incredibly common in our schools, and they are on the rise. In fact, 11 percent of students will be suspended at some point in their school career.[51] But a growing number of people are questioning whether suspensions are an effective form of discipline.

A 2013 editorial in the *New York Times* said that an attempt to combat the rising rates of juvenile crime of the 1980s and school violence incidents like the

Columbine massacre prompted a shift in the way discipline was handled at school.

"One unfortunate result has been the creation of a repressive environment in which young people are suspended, expelled, or even arrested over minor misbehaviors—like talking back or disrupting class—that would once have been handled by the principal," wrote *The Times* Editorial Board.[52]

This increase in suspensions has had some seriously unintended consequences. Suspensions resulted in lower academic outcomes and tended to be discriminatory, with Latino and African-American students receiving a disproportionate number of suspensions. According to data collected by the Department of Education, black students, for example, make up only 16 percent of public school students, but receive 42 percent of suspensions, and they are three times more likely to be expelled than white students. When a student receives a suspension or expulsion, the likelihood they will end up in contact with the juvenile justice system is three-fold.[53] Once students have entered into the juvenile justice system, they are more likely to have subsequent contact with the adult justice system. This phenomenon is known as the school-to-prison pipeline.

Falling back onto suspension-based disciplinary systems put in place for dealing with student behavior instead of addressing situations as they arise may be easier for school officials, but can last in resulting consequences for students. One method recommended by advocates for reducing suspensions is restorative justice. Restorative justice is an excellent example of how practicing empathy and unconditional positive regard with students can lead to better outcomes.

What is restorative justice? Restorative justice, on the most basic level, is a way for students and teachers to work out conflicts through conversation and connection. If, for example, two students got into a fight, the restorative justice process would include facilitating a conversation between the two students about events leading up to the incident, feelings about the incident, and ways to resolve the situation. This is a process that seeks to value the school community, promote empathy and responsibility among students, and put the focus on connection instead of isolation.[54, 55]

Restorative justice is one example of how an empathetic, human-centered approach to discipline can have positive outcomes. In one study,[56] researchers developed an "empathetic condition" among teachers by engaging them in a 70-minute intervention that included sharing stories from student perspectives and providing evidence about the benefits of positive teacher-student relationships, and, while the teachers were not told to stop disciplining students who demonstrated negative or disruptive behaviors, they were given information regarding how developing empathy and maintaining positive relationships with students can help develop their growth. The teachers were also asked to participate in self-reflection. Another group of teachers, not in the "empathetic condition," were given no information. The researchers then examined specific outcomes in the class. The results were shocking. For students of the teachers who experienced the empathetic conditioning, suspensions went down by half. Further, students who had previously experienced suspensions reported they felt more respected by their teachers.[57]

WRAP-UP: EMPATHY WORTH THE EFFORT

Practicing empathy can be really difficult. There are moments when every teacher lets frustration get the best of them, and we understand that. But, the evidence is clear that making efforts to practice and model empathy and unconditional positive regard in your classroom can make a big difference. This doesn't mean you don't discipline, it doesn't mean you let students get away with behaviors without consequences, and it doesn't mean you won't feel frustration. It's okay to be frustrated! Be frustrated at the situation. Be frustrated with the behavior. But understand that children are collections of their experiences and, almost always, behaviors are a coping mechanism. So don't be frustrated at the child. Instead, offer them support. Find ways to meet students—even the most challenging ones—with empathy and love, and you will see those efforts manifest in better behaviors, stronger relationships, and joy at school for you and your students, This change will pave the way for growth mindsets to emerge, as the emphasis moves from dealing with behaviors to supporting learning and growth.

8

PLAY 8: FOSTERING A HAPPY, COLLABORATIVE CLASSROOM

When a flower doesn't bloom, you fix the environment in which it grows, not the flower.

—Alexander Den Heijer

Whoever said Disney World was the happiest place on Earth obviously never had a chance to visit Google headquarters. When we think of office complexes, many people think of cement buildings filled with oppressive cubicle farms illuminated by harsh florescent lighting, but Google takes a different approach to work environments. From sprawling green spaces to scooters and bikes, from putting greens and indoor jungles to comfy couches and collaborative spaces, Google is known for its wonderfully wacky work environments that seek to foster creativity and collaboration, which they claim help boost productivity and job satisfaction. If coming to school every day is the work of our students, don't we want them ensconced in an environment that fosters creativity and collaboration? Providing students the place and space to connect and collaborate creates an environment in which students can learn about themselves and each other. Investing in creating happy, collaborative classrooms means making an investment in the social capital of your school—that is to say, investing in relationships that make our classroom experiences richer and more fulfilling. In this chapter, we're going to figure out how we can deliver a happy, collaborative classroom to our students, and why we should. (Hint: It's because they deserve it!)

THE CLASSROOM PECKING ORDER

You might not think teachers can learn much about happy, collaborative classrooms from chickens, but you'd be wrong. William Muir, a genetics professor and researcher at Purdue University, devised a study to examine the idea of breeding for desirable traits—eugenics, in a word—by conducting an experiment with chickens. The idea was simple: Muir selected out the most productive hens from their flocks (in the world of chickens, productivity is measured by egg production) to create a new flock of super-producers. At the same time, he chose a random flock of chickens and left them alone for several generations. Selecting out these "superchickens" would ideally create a sort of superflock, which would test the theory that selecting out the most desirable members of the group and breeding for high-quality traits would result in a better class of chicken.

But the hypothesis, as it turned out, was wrong.

Several generations of chickens down the road, the group of chickens who had been left to their own devices was flourishing. Group productivity was up 160 percent and the chickens were fat, healthy, and fully feathered. The fate of the superchickens, on the other hand, was not so happy. The three remaining superchickens (six had been murdered by other hens in the flock) had plucked themselves nearly bare and were subjected to a near-constant barrage of attacks from one another.

But why?

"The most productive hen in each cage was the biggest bully, who achieved her productivity by suppressing the productivity of the other hens," wrote Muir. "Bullying behavior is a heritable trait, and several generations were sufficient to produce a strain of psychopaths."[58]

CEO and writer Margaret Heffernan described the experiment and its results in her TED Talk, "Forget the Pecking Order at Work."[59] She paralleled Muir's results to workplace productivity, saying superchickens are much like superstars at work. Heffernan argues that we have been using the superchicken model in business, organizations, and even societies for some time, believing that choosing the very best and brightest means more productivity.

"We've thought that success is achieved by picking the superstars, the brightest men, or occasionally women, in the room, and giving them all the resources and all the power," said Heffernan. "And the result has been just the same as in William Muir's experiment: aggression, dysfunction, and waste."

In the same way, teachers often give their resources to the superchickens of the classroom. Studies have shown that teachers set higher expectations for students they believe to be smart, call on them more often in class, and speak to them more often, with more warmth and affection.[60] This behavior of selecting for superchickens in the classroom and giving them more of our resources, time, and attention breeds competition among our students. Schools are no strangers to competition. Students are constantly ranked against one another by grade and performance, or singled out as valedictorian, honor roll recipient, or student of the month. But is all this competition healthy?

In this competition-driven environment, which many would call the "traditional" classroom, high-performing students are rewarded on individual achievements, singled out for stellar performances, and raised up as examples of good behavior, intelligence, and leadership. But this model often breeds fixed mindsets. First, the students who are not selected as superstars are often left feeling worthless, stupid, or unimportant. In the competitive classroom, no one celebrates a 72 percent on a test, even if it's up from a 58 percent, so what's the point in trying, the logic might go. Fixed mindsets among these students may prevent them from working hard, attempting new challenges, and may even lead to them giving up on school altogether. On the other hand, the students who are singled out as classroom superstars begin to feel pressured to be the best all the time. School becomes less about growth and more about winning, and if you're winning, that means someone else must lose. These fixed mindsets among the high-achieving students can result in a host of negative effects, from an inability to recover from failure to experiencing depression and anguish when they are outperformed.

So, remember that average flock of chickens—the one that didn't end in a pile of plucked feathers and hen carcasses? What made that group so much more productive than the superchickens? Heffernan argues in her talk that because the chickens were not desperate to outperform the rest by any means necessary, they were able to relax into a routine of working together in harmony. She points to a study at MIT that looked at group dynamics. In this study, researchers brought in hundreds of subjects, divided them into groups, and gave them a difficult problem to solve. They found that the groups who managed to solve the problems had some defining qualities, none of which were the largest quantities of people with high IQs.

- **Group members were given equal time to talk.** There was no one singularly driving the conversation, and no one who was just along for the ride.

- **The group demonstrated social sensitivity.** That is to say, they were attuned to each other's moods and needs. Members of these groups scored highly on a test designed to measure empathy.

- **The group had more women.** Heffernan posited that because women scored higher on the empathy test, groups with more women may have a "doubling down of the empathy quotient."

Using this information, Heffernan came to the conclusion that our social connectedness to one another has deep implications in our work and lives. If school is a reflection of the real world, as many argue it should be, then creating opportunities for students to work together in collaboration, not competition, with one another is key to future success. Heffernan discovered that when group members invest in each other and develop relationships, they will be more likely to ask for help, listen to one another's ideas, and engage in honest, productive conflict. Conversely, if members of a group are simply out for themselves, they fail to build any social capital—which Heffernan describes as "reliance and interdependence that builds trust"—so when the time comes for all hands to be on deck, the organizations who have developed social capital among their team members have all the momentum. She visits places like renowned theater companies and businesses on the cutting edge of innovation, and realizes that it is building social capital, not singling out superstars, and valuing collaboration, not individual performance, that makes all the difference.

"Now we need to redefine leadership as an activity in which conditions are created in which everyone can do their most courageous thinking together," says Heffernan. "Now we need everybody, because it is only when we accept that everybody has value that we will liberate the energy and imagination and momentum we need to create the best beyond measure."

Creating these conditions at school means creating a classroom with growth mindset at its core. In this environment, everyone has something to offer, empathy is a core value, and collaboration, not competition, is heralded as the way to success. In this chapter, we'll talk about building social capital by fostering a happy, collaborative classroom atmosphere through developing relationships, setting individual goals, and creating classroom agreements that foster interdependence.

BUILDING A SENSE OF COMMUNITY

A sense of community in the classroom is key to fostering growth mindset among your students. If they don't feel supported or feel self-conscious in their academic endeavors, students are less likely to tackle new challenges and take risks in their learning. So what do we mean when we say "classroom community"? Picture the first day of school with a new class. As you greet the students at the door, you'll encounter a wide range of attitudes, personalities, styles, values, and beliefs. You'll see students dressed in their back-to-school best unpacking sharpened pencils from their carefully chosen pencil case. You'll see students with bed head and mismatched socks who have that look on their faces that says, "I'd rather be getting a root canal than be at school." You'll meet kids who want to make a great first impression and those who immediately want to test your boundaries. Students come in with their own sets of family issues and varied interests, passions, and hobbies; students whose parents have instilled education as a value at home, and those whose parents are deeply mistrusting of institutions. Funny, short, creative, stylish, silly, dimpled, happy, morose, tenderhearted, defiant—students come to us in every possible way and combination of ways, and it is our job to help them forge connections to build a community of learners. Classrooms are made up of a cross-section of students, and creating a classroom community means finding a way to bring all those competing interests, ideas, and ways of being together.

We suggest a three-part plan for getting your classroom community started off on the right foot:

1. Create opportunities to get to know students and for students to get to know each other.

2. Ask students to set goals or intentions for the year.

3. Create a list of classroom agreements as a group.

Building a classroom community can be tricky, but it must start on day one. We love to start the first day of school by incorporating plenty of getting-to-know-you strategies and team-building games. Not only is it critical that the teacher gets to know his or her students, but that the students get to know each other. In doing this, we lay the foundation upon which solid relationships can be built. Here are a few fun strategies and ideas to get you started.

GET-TO-KNOW-YOU STRATEGIES

STRATEGY IDEA	DESCRIPTION
Similarities and differences	This activity can been done in several ways, such as using a large parachute and having students all take their place around the perimeter of the chute. Students will demonstrate similarities by running to various spots around the parachute to agree with statements such as "I have a dog," "I have been to three states," or "I am a fan of Beyoncé." If they disagree with the statement, they will continue to stand in their place until they hear a statement they agree with, at which time they move. This showcases students' similarities and differences, and gets kids moving.

STRATEGY IDEA	DESCRIPTION
On the bus, off the bus	Designate an area within the classroom or on the playground that will be "the bus." Students get on/in the bus to begin the activity. The facilitator designates each side of the bus as an exit for participants. For example, if you would prefer to tour a museum, you would get off the bus on the right side. If you prefer to go to a sporting event, you need to get off the bus on the left side. Once participants "exit" the bus, the facilitator can give them a directive or question to ponder as a group.
Personal inventory, or daily or weekly journaling	Provide an opportunity for students to journal. This can be personal reflections, a Dear Teacher letter, a response to a quote, or more specific and directed questions to help the teacher gather insight on student interests. At the beginning of the year, allow students to decorate their journal in a way that reflects their personalities.
Connect with students	Greet each student at the door or in the hallway by saying their name followed by high fives, fist bumps, hugs, or handshakes. Make a point to use body language to show students that you are happy to see them and they are welcome in the classroom.
Team approach	Replace the pronoun "I" with "we." Make sure your language is inclusive. The team approach helps build positive interdependence in the classroom.
Be transparent, share a story	Share an appropriate personal story with students. A time you struggled, a mistake you made, how you learned something new, a misconception, or a success you have had. Opening up with students and sharing your human side helps them better relate to you.

You may get some eye-rolls at first—especially from older students—but taking the time to incorporate opportunities for students to learn more about you and each other is essential in building a community of learners. As students reveal interesting details about themselves and their interests, make sure to celebrate their similarities and differences. Make an effort to connect students to peers with whom they have things in common, and don't forget to make connections between students' interests and your own. If you find a fellow *Dr. Who* fanatic in your classroom, make a mental note to use that mutual interest to forge a deeper relationship as the year progresses.

ESTABLISHING FLUID GOALS

Roman philosopher Seneca wrote, "When a man does not know what harbor he is making for, no wind is the right wind." In other words, all the favorable conditions in the world don't truly make a difference unless we have an understanding of where we intend to aim. Goals may come in many forms. They may be purely academic ("I want to learn long division"). They may be social goals ("I want to make a new friend"), or they may have to do with character ("I want to be a better listener"). But getting the goals down on paper must be the first step in a student's pursuit of them.

Goal-setting will be more difficult for some students than for others. Many students will come into your classroom without a clear idea of what it is they want to accomplish there, or with the belief they will not accomplish anything at all. Helping students set goals early is key to establishing a classroom community. It's important for students to understand that the goals they set now, in the first weeks of school, may morph over time. They may look different in October and April, and that is a good thing. Allowing students to set fluid goals, monitor their progress, and reposition their desired outcomes over time is essential in creating a community of learners. If we don't allow for growth to change our minds and hearts, then we are stifling our students. Here are some strategies for helping students set goals:

Write it down and keep it.	Once students have crafted a clear, well-written goal, have them tape it to their desktop or the front of their folder to be reminded of it each day.
Share goals with others.	Have students pair up and share their goals so they see what other students are aiming for. This may spark ideas for goals among students, and promote accountability for achieving goals.
Write SMART goals.	Write SMART goals (specific, measurable, attainable, realistic, timely) with students so they can think out the process of accomplishing a goal from beginning to end and have a measurable plan for achievement.
Chunk it into manageable parts.	If students identified a really big goal, help them break it down into manageable parts. Have them "chunk" the task by setting smaller, more manageable goals.

DEVELOPING CLASSROOM AGREEMENTS

The final beginning-of-the-year procedure will be establishing classroom agreements. Make sure your students have written their goals before you begin discussing your agreements. Ask your students what they will need from the teacher and peers to make their goals a reality. Unlike rules, which are often mandated in a top-down fashion, agreements are agreed-upon codes of conduct formulated by the students. In an effort to offer some parameters for classroom agreements, we recommend providing some guidelines.

- Decide on some categories into which the agreements might fall. For example, you might instruct students to only adopt agreements that fall under the categories of Kindness & Respect, Work Ethic, and Personal Responsibility.

- Try to avoid inconsequential or silly rules like "Only two restroom breaks per day" or "Everyone wears pink on Wednesday." Agreements should be big-picture stuff only.

- Once the agreements are made, consider packaging them into a mission statement for your classroom. Refer to it often.

The agreements are more than just run-of-the-mill classroom rules and recommendations. They matter deeply! This act of thoughtfully envisioning a classroom ecosystem with a clear, common set of values and principles is one of the most important things your community of learners will undertake, and it sets the stage upon which the process of learning and growth will unfold each day. One teacher we know developed a set of homework agreements—the students literally created guidelines for what good homework looked like—and saw a huge increase in the number of students turning in homework, and in the quality of returned assignments, too.

Remember the superchickens? Unlike the regular chickens, the superchickens were unsuccessful as a working group because they failed to build social capital. The classroom agreements can serve to augment the development of social capital among your community of learners, particularly when all parties value the established agreements and make efforts to hold themselves and one another accountable to them.

RELIABILITY MATTERS

At the core of social capital is trust. There's an old adage in education, though we cannot pinpoint its origin, that says "students don't care how much you know, until they know how much you care." As we worked through developing content for this book, we kept coming back to the value of relationships in the classroom. Virtually all of the ideas we share in this book are enhanced, if not made possible, by strong relationships.

Where stable teacher-student relationships are built, growth mindsets can flourish. These relationships must be built on a foundation of trust. Students may warm up quickly to a teacher who seems gregarious and caring, but if it becomes apparent the warmth is inauthentic, fixed mindsets emerge. Likewise, students may initially be turned off by a teacher who seems rigorous and inflexible, but may come to find the teacher a stalwart of their education and well-being who is deeply compassionate when the moment calls for it. The point is, authentic relationships take time to develop, and if they aren't built on trust they will quickly disintegrate.

Have you heard of the famous marshmallow test? Stanford psychologist Walter Mischel devised an experiment in the 1970s in which preschool-aged children are put alone in an observation room with a researcher who puts a delicious, fluffy marshmallow in front of them.[61] The researcher informs the child that he or she may eat the marshmallow now, or, if he or she is willing to wait to eat the marshmallow until the researchers returns, they'll get a second marsh-mallow, too. If they eat the first marshmallow, they won't get a second. Then the researcher leaves the child and the marshmallow in the room to observe through a two-way mirror.

Of course, all manner of hilarity ensues. The kids find funny ways to engage themselves so as not to think about the marshmallow, like singing songs or fidgeting. One nibbles the bottom of the marshmallow and returns it to the plate in a way that obscures the offending bite marks. Some opt for the "out of sight, out of mind" theory and sit on the marshmallow. And, of course, some succumb to temptation and gobble it up. The experiment was designed to study how children delay gratification and exhibit self-control and willpower. Researchers then followed the children as they grew, and discovered those who were able to wait to receive the second marshmallow—the kids who exhibited self-control and managed to delay gratification—tended to have better life outcomes in the future.

Of course, the marshmallow test has its detractors, with many saying it is more a referendum on the child's view of authority than it is an indicator of their self-control.[62] A study released in 2012 revealed that the results of the marshmallow test may have more to do with environmental influences than it does with inborn willpower.

Celeste Kidd, a researcher at the University of Rochester, devised an experiment that would evaluate if environmental influences affect the outcomes of the marshmallow test.[63] The researchers divided the preschool-aged subjects into two groups. But before the marshmallow test commenced, all the children were given an activity where they could decorate a paper cup.

In the first group of children, the researchers wanted to create an unreliable condition. So, they offered a box of used crayons to the children with which to decorate the cups. Then, they said if the child could wait, they would go get a better set of art supplies with which the children could work. After a few minutes, the researcher returned empty-handed saying, "I'm sorry, but I made a mistake. We don't have any other art supplies after all." The children were directed to use the old crayons. Then a single sticker was placed on the table, and the researcher told the child they would go get some more stickers. Again, the researcher turned up empty handed explaining they must have run out. In the second group, reliability was established as the researchers delivered on both their promises of new art supplies and more stickers.

After setting up the reliable and unreliable environments, the marshmallow test commenced. It was the same scenario: The child could eat the marshmallow immediately, or wait 15 minutes for the researcher to bring back a second.

In the first group—the unreliable environment—the average wait time before eating the marshmallow was three minutes. In the second group—the reliable environment—the average wait time was 12 minutes. Only 1 out of the 14 children in the unreliable conditions waited the entire 15 minutes to get the second marshmallow, while 9 of the 14 in the reliable conditions waited out the clock. So what does this study show us? That the level of trust and reliability in a given environment make for a substantial difference in outcomes.

Ask yourself if your classroom is a place of trust and reliability. Do you often do what you'll say? Do you frequently renege on promises to your students? Making an effort to be mindful of behaviors that undermine the reliability quotient of the classroom will make a difference in outcomes.

WRAP-UP: HAPPY STUDENTS = BETTER OUTCOMES

How are you making efforts to make your classroom a happier place? Do a self-reflection by honestly answering the following questions about the classroom environment you have established.

How do I encourage play in my classroom?

_____

_____

_____

How do I encourage creativity and wonder?

_____

_____

_____

How do I encourage self-discovery among my students?

_____

_____

_____

How do I give opportunities for collaborative work?

_____

_____

_____

In what ways have I created a comfortable environment in the classroom? (Can they move around the room freely? Is there flexible seating?)

_____

_____

_____

How do I include students in analyzing their own data and tracking their progress as learners?

_____

_____

_____

What specific ways do I build social capital in my classroom?

_____

_____

_____

How do I make efforts to foster trust, reliability, and interdependence in my classroom?

_____

_____

_____

How do I describe the overall tone and mood of my classroom?

_____

_____

_____

If you identified areas that need improvement, seek out resources and mentors to help foster positive ideals in your classroom that can help make it a happier place. Educational researchers have begun to study the implications of happiness in the classroom, and the early results indicate that happier students tend to have better academic outcomes.[64] Try asking your students what they love most about school, and they will likely say something about playing or socializing with their friends. When you foster strong relationships and friendships in your classrooms, your students will have more positive experiences in the learning environment. Likewise, if you ask teachers what they love most about school, they will likely point to their students. So it makes sense to invest in quality teacher-student and peer-to-peer relationships and building social capital; that investment may very well pay dividends.

9

PLAY 9: INCREASING ENGAGEMENT

Tell me and I forget, teach me and I may
remember, involve me and I learn.

—Benjamin Franklin

When Carly was in fifth grade, science was the most exciting part of the day. Her teacher, Ms. Fisher, had a flair for creating engaging science lessons from raising monarch butterflies to growing mold in petri dishes to making all manner of things fizz, bubble, and explode. Carly knew that science meant fun, and fun, in this case, meant learning. Cut to high school chemistry lab, where Carly lumbers in just ahead of the bell and wills herself not to fall asleep for 90 excruciating minutes. The labs are complicated and rarely as enjoyable as anything Ms. Fisher taught. There are lots of notes, slideshows, and terms to memorize. And, like many high school students, Carly has made the decision to mentally check out.

Boredom in high school is nothing new. According to the 2013 Annual Gallup Student Poll, which surveys nearly a half-million American students, just 4 out of every 10 high school students say they feel engaged at school.[65] In elementary school, that number is 8 out of 10 students. So what happens between fifth grade and high school that leaves students like Carly feeling uninspired by and disengaged from their education? In this chapter, we're going to look at some evidence-based strategies for increasing engagement at school that seek to offer students more engaging, impactful learning experiences.

A BETTER WAY

Jal Mehta and Sarah Fine of the Harvard Graduate School of Education were studying "powerful learning"—deep learning experiences that particularly resonate with students—in schools when they began to notice something significant happening in American classrooms.[66] In the core classes like math, science, and history, the learning was often teacher-centered—the teacher was the main event, while the students served as spectators with the occasional audience participation bit. In the teacher-centered classroom, the students' job is most often to take notes, do assigned work, and answer questions when asked. Conversely, the researchers noted that when students attended their elective classes and extracurricular clubs—the classes they chose to join, like music, debate, and art—they were far more engaged. The students were eagerly participating, the researchers noted, and even seeking out leadership roles in these classes and clubs. So, Mehta and Fine wanted to know, what made the difference?

The researchers uncovered a number of ways the experiences students were having in these "peripheral spaces" (the term they used to refer to electives and extracurricular activities) differed from their experiences in the core classes. Here's what they discovered about the peripheral spaces:

- Students *chose* to be part of the peripheral educational experiences; they were mandated to enroll in the core classes.

- There were lots of opportunities for teamwork, and less emphasis was placed on individual achievement.

- There were many opportunities to take on leadership roles and work with peers in a learning capacity (e.g., students could teach to and learn from each other).

- The activities often echoed the values of American culture outside of the classroom (e.g., sports, music, politics, etc.).

Mehta and Fine argued that in a class like musical theater, for example, students had the opportunity to build their own production from the initial casting to taking a bow on performance night, whereas in the core classes, they would not get the same opportunity to wholly experience this production process; it is unlikely high school students would develop a mathematical theorem or uncover a scientific breakthrough while at school. The researchers refer to this style of education in periphery spaces as "apprenticeship learning," or learning through doing. Often, the teachers of these elective subjects were themselves students of the craft. It wouldn't be uncommon for an art teacher to have a gallery opening on the weekend, separate from her schoolwork, or find a music teacher singing in a local choral group, or a band teacher jamming out in a local rock band. You would be more hard-pressed to find a math teacher working as a mathematician on the side, or a biology teacher working to cure a disease in her spare time. This role as a learner of the craft outside of the school, the researchers theorized, helped the teachers to keep their perspectives fresh and develop empathy for and better identify with other learners of the craft.

As they began to develop these understandings of the differences between the core and periphery classes, Mehta and Fine noted the most powerful core classes were those in which the teacher organized the learning around the production of an authentic experience. The most effective teachers were not the ones who taught the most content, but rather the ones who helped students acquire the mindset of someone in the discipline. This approach seemed to better engage students with the content. Mehta and Fine also argue that student choice factors into engagement: When students get to engage in learning through a topic that appeals to them, engagement increases. They also offer this final piece of advice: "Most importantly, the ethos of these classrooms is similar to what one might find at an athletic practice or theater rehearsal—an ethos that combines playfulness with purposefulness, drawing together the warm virtue of passion and interest with the cooler virtues of intellectual demand."

Thinking about Mehta and Fine's observations, consider how you can draw in elements from the electives and extracurricular activities that students choose to take in order to increase engagement in your own classroom. Complete the following self-inquiry as you reflect on your classroom practice.

RAISING ENGAGEMENT: A SELF-INQUIRY

QUESTION	REFLECTION
"Apprenticeship learning" gives students an opportunity to learn through experience. What is an authentic experience of a person working in the discipline I teach? How can I bring that experience into my classroom in a way that meets my academic objectives and gives students a fulfilling, authentic experience?	
Students feel more engaged in their learning when they are given choice. How can I allow students to tap into their diverse interests and passions while still attaining my learning objective?	
How can I become a student of my craft? Could I take an online class or challenge myself to learn something new in my discipline in order to have an experience that helps me identify with my students? Could I create a learning experience for my students in which I can also participate as a learner?	
If I think of myself as a coach of this learning team, how can I get my team to have fun while also learning? What are some non-negotiable academic objectives that might be difficult for students to navigate? How can I temper that difficulty with a sense of enjoyment and fun?	

Consider for a moment why students engage with extracurricular activities and electives differently than core classes by reflecting on your own experience. Many of us can recount stories from childhood of hours spent perfecting a jump shot or dragging ourselves out of bed at 6 AM on a Saturday to attend a debate tournament. Consider what motivated you to go the extra mile for your extra-curricular activities, and then think about ways you might be able to harness that energy in your classroom.

THE BEYOND-AVERAGE TEACHER

The opposite of bored, says Harvard professor Todd Rose, is not entertained: it's engaged.[67] It's easy to get the two confused. If you have ever tried to teach a historical event through video games or written and performed a rap about Shakespeare, you may have thought you were engaging your students, when all you were really doing was keeping them briefly entertained. So, what is engagement exactly? We've developed this simple working definition: Engagement is student connection to a learning experience evidenced by wholehearted participation.

As we think about creating engaging, authentic learning experiences, many teachers (and we're including ourselves in this assessment!) fall victim to designing an experience for the "average" student, instead of developing an experience that is open-ended in a way that allows it to resonate with individual learners in unique and meaningful ways.

Rose has spent a lot of time researching society's obsession with averages—he wrote a book on the topic, *The End of Average: How We Succeed in a World that Values Sameness*—and argues that many of our institutions are built with the average in mind. He uses a story from the Air Force to illustrate this point.[68]After noticing an uptick in pilots having difficulty controlling the planes in the 1950s, the Air Force decided that their standardized cockpit, initially designed in the 1920s, was just too small. The average size of a pilot had increased, so the small cockpit design was leading to pilot errors. The Air Force decided to build a cockpit for the larger 1950s pilot, and so undertook measuring 4,000 pilots on 10 dimensions (height, weight, chest circumference, etc.), and from that data derived the measurement in each dimension of an averaged-sized pilot, with the belief that most pilots would fall into average range on most dimensions.

But that's not what happened. None of the pilots fell into the average range in all 10 categories. And when they tried to find pilots who were "average" in just three categories, only a little over 3 percent fit the bill. They realized that the pilots came in all shapes and sizes. Some had long arms, but short legs. Some were short with barrel chests. Average just didn't seem to apply. So, instead of building to the "average," which the Air Force quickly learned was exactly no one, they forced manufacturers to find a way to suit the individual differences of their pilots. All of sudden, cockpits started featuring things like adjustable seats.

Rose draws a parallel between the Air Force and today's modern system of education, and says we need to apply the flexibility of the fighter jet's cockpit to the classroom. When we create an environment designed for an "average" learner, we ultimately let a lot of kids slip through the cracks. Rose argues that people have "jagged" profiles, meaning we are good at some things and less so in others; we can quickly catch on to some subjects, but struggle with others. "If we ignore jaggedness, we end up treating people in one-dimensional terms," says Rose.[69]

Rose says that one solution to the problem of "average" would be creating a fluid classroom environment that fits each student, instead of forcing students to fit into a single classroom environment. Rose was once a high-school kid with a 0.9 GPA before he dropped out altogether. Why? Because, according to him, he didn't fit. As he began to understand the "jaggedness" of his own profile, he was able to find success by utilizing his strongest attributes, and by understanding and developing strategies to account for his shortcomings.

Indeed, disabusing oneself of the notion of "average" is central to success in the growth-oriented classroom, but in a profession often focused on standardization, there are systemic obstacles to honoring the individuality of our students. Letting go of the idea of a "normal" or "typical" student allows the teacher to start thinking in terms of open-ended learning experiences to which students can bring different passions and skills, and from which they can benefit in a variety of ways.

THE SINGLE-POINT RUBRIC

Let's say Mr. Jackson has an awesome idea for a group project. He feels motivated by his idea and he's sure the kids in his class will love collaborating and digging into this project. He sits down to start putting his rubric together and very quickly, his enthusiasm for the project begins to wane. Further, he knows as soon as he hands out this rubric, his students' enthusiasm will evaporate, too. He's produced something that looks like this:

Research Paper Rubric
English 10
Instructor: Annie Brock

Group Members _____ Topic _____

	10/9	8/7/6	5/4/3	2/1
Research Portfolio	The portfolio is neat, organized, and in order with dividers in place.	The portfolio is somewhat neat, organized, and in order with most dividers in place.	The portfolio is somewhat disorganized, with several dividers absent or out of place.	The portfolio is disorganized with dividers absent.
Introduction/ Thesis Statement	Author writes an attention-catching introduction, and a thoughtful, engaging thesis statement.	Author writes a somewhat attention-catching introduction, and somewhat thoughtful, engaging thesis statement.	Author writes an introduction and thesis, though they are not engaging and lacking in thoughtfulness.	Introduction and thesis statement are absent or incomplete.
Organization	Three claims and each point are clear and related to the thesis.	Three claims and each point are somewhat clear and mostly related to the thesis	Three claims and each point are somewhat unclear and unrelated to the thesis.	Three claims and each point are missing or completely unclear or unrelated to the thesis.
Using Evidence to Support Thinking	Evidence chosen shows excellent critical thinking skills, including inferences, synthesis, and connections to outside world.	Every topic sentence/main idea is clearly supported with evidence or examples to support thinking	Topic sentences/main ideas are not clearly stated and/or are not supported with specific examples	There is little or no evidence to support thinking
Analysis	Student carefully analyzed the information collected and drew appropriate conclusions supported by evidence.	Conclusions drawn in paper shows student made effort to analyze the evidence collected	Student's conclusions needs support from stronger evidence. Levels of analysis could have been more in depth.	Student's conclusions from research simply involved restating information or the evidence did not support student's conclusion.
Transitions	A variety of thoughtful transitions are used. They clearly show how ideas are connected.	Transitions clearly show how ideas are connected, but there is little variety.	Some transitions work well, but connections between other ideas are fuzzy.	The transitions between ideas are unclear or non-existent.
Conclusion	Conclusion addresses the points of the thesis and reviews topics of paper without too much repetition and ends with something impactful.	Conclusion is present but does address the complete thesis and does not end with an impactful statement.	Conclusion is present but not strongly written and does not follow outline.	Conclusion is barely present if present at all. Does not follow outline.
Paper, Title, Page Numbers Header.	Correct MLA formatting/ thoughtful title	Somewhat correct MLA formatting/ somewhat thoughtful title	MLA formatting is mostly incorrect/title is present, but not well thought out	MLA formatting is totally incorrect and title is absent
Grammar and Mechanics	Author makes no grammar errors that distract the reader from the content.	Author makes 1-3 grammar errors that distract the reader from the content.	Author makes 4-6 grammar errors that distract the reader from the content.	Author makes more than 6 grammar errors that distract the reader from the content.
Spelling and Word Choice	All words are spelled correctly and student uses varied and appropriate word choice.	Most words are spelled correctly, and student uses somewhat varied word choice.	Several words are spelled incorrectly and student uses somewhat poor word choice.	Many words are spelled incorrectly and student uses poor word choice.
Sentence Fragments and Run-ons	All sentences are complete.	1-2 run-on sentences or sentence fragments.	3-4 run-on sentences or sentence fragments.	More than 4 run-on sentences or sentence fragments.
Format: In-Text Citations and Works Cited	Works Cited page formatted correctly and in-text citations are appropriately used.	Works cited page has a few formatting errors and in-text citations are generally used correctly.	Works cited page has multiple formatting errors and in-text citations are mostly used incorrectly.	Works cited page has absent or completely incorrect. In-text citations are absent or incorrectly used.

Total: _____ /120

Yes, dear reader, this rubric is supposed to be fuzzy and undecipherable because we like you, and we don't want you to endure reading it. It's a real rubric once used by one of us. Yikes!

That's a pretty detailed rubric, and it's easy to see how it could quickly narrow the playing field in terms of the kind of work that is considered acceptable. Now, what if Mr. Jackson took into account Todd Rose's thoughts on the jaggedness of people? What if instead of trying to come up with a comprehensive list of all the ways a student might go right or wrong in finishing the project, he left it as open-ended as possible so his students could bring their own ideas, talents, and creativity to the table? That's when he stumbled on the single-point rubric.

Analytic rubrics have become a staple in the American classroom. It's a noble idea, providing detailed guidelines on how students can demonstrate their mastery of a certain skill. In theory, these rubrics take largely subjective grading (like projects and papers) and establish clear criteria for success. But somewhere along the way, these rubrics became so loaded down with detail that they stopped serving both the student and teacher. The teacher spends large amounts of time crafting the rubric, and the student's eyes glaze over when they receive it. If the student reads the rubric at all, it's to zero in on the "meets the standard" or "exceeds the standard" categories so they can quickly figure out the bottom line without having to wade through loads of unnecessary detail.

Rubrics like this also illustrate a top-down approach to learning that prescribes a "right" way to do a task, activity, or assignment. But we know there are lots of ways to approach a topic and demonstrate mastery. Detailed rubrics do not value a multi-dimensional approach to learning; rather, they pinpoint a single stratagem for success and provide a single pathway for achieving it. It's easy to see how an analytic rubric might squash student creativity, as students are so busy literally trying to fit their work in a tiny box that there is little room for improvisation. A growth-mindset approach would be to create guidelines that provide multiple pathways to success. Enter the single-point rubric.

A single-point rubric identifies the performance criteria, but also allows for teacher-student conferencing, feedback for improvement, and evidence for how the student meets the criteria. Unlike the analytic rubric, there is no limit to achievement. Exemplary work can be demonstrated in a variety of areas, not just the specific ways the teacher has devised that a student can demonstrate mastery. Likewise, the teacher doesn't have to think of all the ways a student can fail to meet or exceed the standard; instead, the teacher can use the saved time for student conferences to check in during the process and on the back end of the project to provide useful, relevant feedback to the student.

So, let's get back to Mr. Jackson's great idea. He's decided to have his students work in groups to create podcasts in which they "interview" a historical figure. Instead of overkill on all the requirements of the podcasts, he invites creativity by keeping the rules to a minimum. His single-point rubric has a "Not Yet" column for offering constructive feedback to students who fell short of the standard, and "Evidence" and "Advanced" columns for describing how the criteria was met or exceeded. It looks like this:

SINGLE-POINT RUBRIC

NOT YET Areas that need improvement	CRITERIA Standards of performance	EVIDENCE How the criteria was met	ADVANCED Areas that were above and beyond
	Performance Students' voices are clear, the podcast follows a loose script, and all students are included in the production of the podcast.		
	Content Includes thought-provoking questions and answers based on factual people, places, and events. Conversation stays on topic. The podcast includes a brief introduction and conclusion that engages the listener.		
	Production The length is manageable and keeps the listener engaged. The production value is such that all voices are understood clearly, the volume is reasonable, and relevant musical cues and other sounds are included.		

Isn't that better? His students still have guidelines. They know what must be included in the podcast, and Mr. Jackson has a springboard from which to provide detailed feedback on the project. Take a moment to identify a project or task that you currently use an analytic rubric to assess. Try your hand at filling out this blank single-point rubric for it instead.[70]

NOT YET Areas that need improvement	CRITERIA Standards of performance	EVIDENCE How the criteria was met	ADVANCED Areas that were above and beyond
	Mastery Criteria #1: Description of performance quality		
	Mastery Criteria #2: Description of performance quality		
	Mastery Criteria #3: Description of performance quality		

MULTI-DIMENSIONAL TEACHING AND LEARNING

We know that students who possess a strong growth mindset have positive academic outcomes, but less is known about how the mindsets, both fixed and growth, develop inside the classroom. Researcher Dr. Kathy Liu Sun found, in the course of her doctoral research, that when mathematics teachers took a multi-dimensional approach to the subject—that is to say, they approached it with the assumption there are many ways to "do" math and solve math problems—the teachers communicated growth-mindset messages to their students and the students took on a similar multi-dimensional approach to learning math.[71] On the other hand, teachers who had a one-dimensional approach to math (the assumption that there is one right way to solve a problem) often communicated fixed messages to their students. The superior outcomes of the multi-dimensional approach indicated that growth-mindset messaging in mathematics bolstered student progress.

As the author of *Mathematical Mindsets*, Jo Boaler, writes on her website, youcubed .com: "Mathematics is a beautiful, open, creative, and multi-dimensional subject. But school mathematics is often uninspiring, procedural, and one-dimensional—it's all about memorizing methods and procedures."[72]

Boaler argues that real-world math is far from one-dimensional, and that often the math taught in schools is not reflective of how math is utilized in the 21st-century workplace. But this argument might be applied to several other disciplines outside of math, as well. Making efforts to inspire curiosity in your classroom and fostering many pathways to success is the mark of a multi-dimensional teacher.

Psychology professor George Slavich coined the term "transformational teaching."[73] Slavich talked about his own educational journey, in which he entered college believing that he would major in business. When no business under-graduate program was offered, he switched to economics. Halfway through his economics course with a decidedly uninspiring teacher, he decided it wasn't for him. On a lark, he enrolled in a psychology class with a friend, where he encountered John Gabrieli. Gabrieli made Slavich's introductory psychology class endlessly interesting and presented topics in a way that sparked curiosity and a desire to learn more in his students. Slavich switched his major to psychology from economics, but often wondered what might have happened had his economics teacher inspired passion in him the way his psych professor did.

"From that experience I realized that boring teachers alienate students not only from learning about a specific topic area, but even worse, they run the risk of alienating students from learning in general," wrote Slavich in an essay titled *On Becoming a Teacher of Psychology*. "Passionate teachers have the opposite effect: They transform something fundamental inside of their students in order to foster a passion for continued learning."

A one-dimensional approach to teaching rarely inspires curiosity and wonder. Passion for a subject develops when students feel engaged, and nothing squashes engagement faster than a singular, close-minded approach to learning. Consider experimenting with strategies that provoke interest and spark curiosity.

STUDENT ENGAGEMENT STRATEGIES [74, 75]

Share your enthusiasm for learning!	Let students see how excited you are about the lesson and learning. Your positivity and enthusiasm will be contagious.
Lights, camera, action!	Activate student schema with essential questions, a video hook, or an anticipation guide; include opportunities for self-reflection, and engage students in table talk around the concept.
Encourage productive struggle, with support.	Prompt students with questions that lead to students needing to work through tasks or additional research. Be sure to model and explicitly teach students how to move through obstacles.
Integrate technology.	Bring in technology, such as Poll Everywhere, Padlet, or Nearpod, in a purposeful way that enhances the lesson and increases engagement.
Provide collaborative practice and an opportunity to perform or present.	Structure lessons that allow students to collaborate with their peers and perform or present their learning to a relevant audience.
Increase movement in the classroom.	Add actions to help students learn new information, giving students opportunities to move and share. The act of getting up and down, performing actions, and talking will keep their bodies physically engaged and their minds mentally engaged.
Foster positive relationships with your students and build a growth environment for learning.	Students should feel comfortable and welcome in their learning environment. Much of this depends on the way a teacher responds to and behaves toward learners; positive interactions with teachers will lead to increased engagement.
Provide ample wait time after questions and give thoughtful responses and feedback.	Allow a proper wait time for students to devise answers and questions, and use student responses as an opportunity to increase participation with further open-ended questioning. Consider responding with curiosity and interest, additional questions, and growth dialog rather than vague, meaningless responses such as "good job" or "interesting thought."
Check your pace and transitions.	Keep the pace of the lesson moving, but not so quickly that it frustrates learners who require more processing time to connect to the new learning.
Keep it student centered.	Use lab rotations, centers, and small groups to keep the instruction student centered.
Increase purposeful note taking and ways for students to organize their learning.	Explicitly teach, model, and engage students in learning, and use several note-taking models to increase student engagement (e.g., Cornell Notes, foldables, graphic organizers, teacher-prepared notes, sketchnotes).

THE GROWTH MINDSET PLAYBOOK

Turn and teach!	The teacher gives small amounts of information using non-linguistic drawings, gestures, or kinesthetic movements and then says "turn and teach." Students then turn and teach their partner by mimicking the teacher. Example: When teaching the water cycle, include a song with movements. Break the song into small chunks, providing opportunities for students to turn and teach. The focus should be on making progress toward student goals. The students are the drivers of their learning; the teacher is the facilitator.

WRAP-UP: ACKNOWLEDGE AND EMBRACE DIFFERENCES

Education researcher Sir Ken Robinson, known for his passionate speeches and books on education reform, said this: "Human communities depend upon a diversity of talent, not a singular conception of ability."[76] When we create homogenized classrooms, we miss out on cultivating the most important and distinct of the human qualities: curiosity, wonder, and passion. We said before that engagement is student connection to a learning experience evidenced by wholehearted participation. Make efforts each day to connect the material in your class to your students' innate sense of wonder and curiosity. Draw out their wholehearted participation by acknowledging how their differences and specialness as individual people will make the learning experience unique and worthwhile for the entire class.

10

PLAY 10:
MOONSHOTS

Our deepest fear is not that we are inadequate.
Our deepest fear is that we are powerful beyond measure.

—Marianne Williamson

There's this theory that has its roots in technology and space travel called moonshot thinking. To forward thinkers like Larry Page, one of the founders of Google, moonshot thinking is sacrosanct. It is part and parcel of every worthwhile achievement made in history, and it is the bedrock on which Page and his cohorts have built incredible, unthinkable technological advancements. In the past 10 years, we've seen the technology industry take off and change the world in innumerable ways. Meanwhile, today's education model looks frighteningly similar to the way it did 50 years ago. Larry Page once said, "Always work hard on something uncomfortably exciting." Educators, it's time to get out of our comfort zone and set our sights on the moon.

WHAT IS A MOONSHOT?

X, formerly Google X, is a research and development outfit founded by Google that focuses on making 10x (ten times) improvements—that is, instead of trying to make incremental progress at, say, 10 percent, the mission of X is to make 10x advancements. Consider the Space Race of the 1960s as an example. When President John F. Kennedy declared the United States was going to be the first to put a man on the moon, he truly had no idea how it was going to be accomplished. But once the goal was laid out, people rallied around the idea and, in just 10 short years, made it a reality. Moonshots like these, as X describes them, "live in the gray area between audacious technology and pure science fiction." Moonshot thinking inspired John F. Kennedy to utter the famed words, "We do things not because they are easy, but because they are hard."

So, what does moonshot thinking look like in our schools? Can you imagine what lives in the gray area between audacious education and pure science fiction? And how can you inspire the moonshot mindset in your students? These are the young people who will one day grow up to be the Larry Pages and John Glenns of their time, which is why it is critical that, early and often, we reinforce the idea that anything is possible, even the things we have not yet dared to dream. The dreamers are sitting in front of us, looking to us for inspiration, guidance, even permission to think big. And, perhaps, the very best place to start inspiring audacious thinking is by helping our students develop growth mindsets.

THE MOONSHOT MINDSET

Part of adopting the growth mindset as your personal and classroom modus operandi is accepting that you can never really know what the outcomes will be. Knowing, or thinking one knows, begets limitations, and limitations beget fixed mindsets. As Carol Dweck writes in *Mindset*, "A person's true potential is unknown and unknowable. It is impossible to foresee what can be accomplished with years of passion, toil, and training."

The 10 percent teacher doesn't rock the boat. He or she invests time where only small amounts of growth are possible—enough to keep the students passing tests, behaving well, and moving through the system. T.S. Eliot said, "Only those who will risk going too far can possibly find out how far one can go." The 10x teacher is a risk-taker who understands the results may not be as immediate or black-and-white as a test score, but that doesn't really matter because a test score isn't the end game. The 10x teacher ignores the cries of dissent: "The students are too young to understand!" "The status quo isn't ready for change!" "We've always done it this way!" "The administration will never approve!" Instead, they forge ahead and insist on the power of potential in the face of inscrutable outcomes.

Think of moonshot thinking as placing a bet on your students' futures. Indeed, you have placed a very real bet: You've staked your life's work on helping students succeed, so saddling them—or yourself—with limits to their potential for achievement is counterintuitive to the wager you made the moment you took your first teaching job. You remember the one; the wager that said, "I'm here to make a difference." So the question becomes, how can you maximize your potential for the greatest return? In schools, "disruption" is often a dirty word—too much of it, and you'll get sent to the principal's office—but in the larger culture, "disruption" is an innovation that turns the status quo on its head, often making life better, more worthwhile. The education system, it seems, is ripe for disruption.

When you visit the X website (a.k.a. The Moonshot Factory), they offer a Venn diagram that serves as their moonshot blueprint. We've reproduced a version of it in the lesson plan below, but you can check out the original online at x.company.

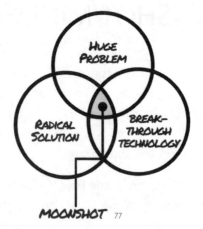

THE GROWTH MINDSET PLAYBOOK

First, the team looks for big problems, problems that impact millions of people. Then, they devise a radical solution, one thought to be impossible using only what tools are available today. Many of the solutions, they say, seem more like science fiction. Next, the X team identifies a current technology, one that may not be exactly what they are looking for, but that offers the promise of realizing the solution in the future. Yes, it sounds crazy, but also totally cool, right? Here are a few of the projects currently underway at X:

Project Loon—A network of balloons hovering in the stratosphere that creates a wireless network, Project Loon aims to provide Internet to billions of people living in remote areas all over the world.

Makani—After identifying inefficiencies in traditional wind turbines, the Makani team developed energy kites that are able to generate more electricity while using less materials to do it.

Project Wing—This project uses automated aircraft (drones) to deliver goods to people, in hopes of cutting back on many of the pollution-causing delivery vehicles on the roadways.

X's website offers information on many of the projects the organization has undertaken, including successful ones like Waymo, a self-driving vehicle project, along with explorations like one that attempted to create fuel from seawater. We've devised a mini-lesson with the aim of getting students to engage in the process of moonshot thinking. But first, a few caveats.

This lesson can be difficult for a number of reasons. We've found that the youngest students—kindergartners and first-grade students who've yet to develop a stifling sense of pragmatism—readily engage in moonshot thinking. But often, older students (and definitely adults!) have trouble thinking in the realm of science fiction that moonshots demand. Like growth mindset, moonshot thinking is a kind of mindset. If students cannot see beyond what currently exists, they will have a hard time devising plans that are currently impossible. Younger students are rarely saddled with the limitations of reality.

In the lesson plan below, we ask you to question your students, guiding them to take the perspective of an ordinary person living in the 1960s and hearing about the idea of putting a man on the moon for the first time. That person must have thought it sounded preposterous! But preposterousness does not stop moonshot thinkers; it invigorates them. And, less than 10 years later, moonshot thinkers, galvanized by the audacious goal to put a man on the moon, turned President Kennedy's dream into a reality. For your more skeptical students, you may want to offer up more of the scenarios of the impossible being made possible. In 1900, the ability to fly likely sounded absurd, but the Wright Brothers did it in 1903. In 1950, people likely thought attempting to summit Mount Everest was nothing more than a death wish, but Sir Edmund Hillary and Sherpa Tenzing Norgay conquered the mountain in 1953 and lived to tell the tale. More recently, in 2000, people likely couldn't conceive of being able to order virtually anything online and have it delivered in two days, but Amazon has made it a reality. Offering up these examples will help the critics open up to engaging with moonshot thinking.

MOONSHOT THINKING

MINI-LESSON

LEARNING OBJECTIVE

At the end of the lesson, students will be able to:

- understand the meaning and significance of moonshot thinking
- demonstrate their ability to develop moonshots using the X formula

RESOURCES AND MATERIALS

- Computer
- Presentation equipment (projector, speakers, etc.)
- Internet access
- X formula Venn diagram

METHOD

SAY: More than 50 years ago, in 1962, President John F. Kennedy stood at a podium at Rice University in Houston, Texas, and while the world was watching, he announced to the crowd that the United States was going to put a man on the moon. (You can find the full speech here: https://go.nasa.gov/2mmq10G.) Today, that doesn't seem like such a radical idea; many astronauts have been to the moon. But in 1962, when President Kennedy announced his plan to put a man on the moon by the end of the decade, it was a big deal. It had never been done before! In fact, President Kennedy said in his speech the technology to do it didn't even exist yet. But nevertheless, he insisted. What do you think people might have said about his plan to put a man on the moon in 1962? (Possible student responses: "You're crazy!""It can't be done!""Let's go for it!")

SAY: Well, guess what? In July of 1969, just six months before time ran out on President Kennedy's promise, Astronaut Neil Armstrong became the first man who walked on the moon. He even planted an American flag there. It was an exciting day for our country. Today, we look back on that time and on President Kennedy's impossible goal of putting a man on the moon as a symbol of innovation and courage. It's a lesson that teaches us anything is possible. I'm going to show you a video about a company working in California that does something called "moonshot thinking," based on President Kennedy's idea to put a man on the moon. (Show video: "What is Moonshot Thinking?" by X, The Moonshot Factory—http://bit.ly/YU1grL.)

SAY: The X company is in the business of moonshot thinking. What I mean by that is that they are working to solve big problems with radical solutions that we don't even have the technology to develop yet. It's kind of like science fiction! Let's take a look at a few of the projects they're working on.

Using a single computer or directing students to use their own devices, navigate to the X website at x.company. Here, you can do a number of things, depending on the ages of your students. For younger students, go the Projects link and discuss some of the projects. Waymo, the driverless car project, might be a good starting place. Have students explore the website or do a teacher-led guided exploration. Then, introduce the Moonshot Thinking Blueprint, developed by X:

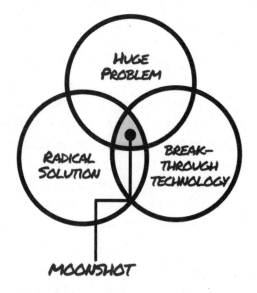

SAY: When X is engaged in moonshot thinking, they use this blueprint. First, they think of a really big problem—one that affects millions or, in some cases, billions of people—then they brainstorm ideas to solve the problem. I'm talking big, seemingly unrealistic ideas. For example, they came up with one idea that tried to use ocean water as a source of fuel. What do you think the huge problem was? (Possible student responses: "We need more fuel for cars." "Oil and gas are bad for the environment." "Oil is a nonrenewable resource, so we need to find new fuel sources.") Right! That's a big problem to solve. So, in this case, what was the solution they came up with? (Student response: "To use water from the oceans to make fuel," or variation.) Yes! Why do you think they chose seawater? (Possible student answers: "There is a lot of it." "We could use it as a source of clean fuel for vehicles and other things." "It could replace the use of fossil fuels, which create pollution and contribute to global warming.") Yes, those are great reasons to explore seawater as a fuel source! After they decided on seawater, they used a process to extract carbon dioxide and hydrogen from the water; that was the break-through technology. Ultimately, while the X team did manage to create fuel from seawater, the process was not cost-effective enough to be a viable solution, so they ended the exploration. Even though they didn't succeed in their exploration, they were thinking big, and they accomplished something that had never been done! That is what moonshot thinking is all about. Would you like to try it?

Distribute a 3-circle Venn diagram or ask students to draw their own on a piece of paper. For the first time, you may want to start by offering students a problem to solve. These might be world issues or even country, city, or school-specific problems, but they should affect many people. We've come up with a list for you to choose from, but we encourage you to include your own or ask students to think up their own big problems to solve later on. Of course, younger students may not be prepared to tackle problems like sex trafficking or drug abuse. Be considerate of the age-appropriate nature of the problems you present. It would be helpful to identify a few resources like videos, articles, etc., that help explain the problem to students if they're unfamiliar with it.

Thinking Globally

- 100,000 animals die every year from plastic bags.

- Football players are increasingly suffering traumatic brain injuries from playing the game.

- 32 million girls around the world do not have access to school.

- Honeybees are experiencing a high rate of decline across the globe.

- In the United States, there are approximately 1.5 million homeless people.

Thinking Locally

- Many children in our community cannot afford music lessons.

- Some students have to ride the bus for over 90 minutes each day.

- Produce at our local grocery store is more expensive than processed foods.

- It is difficult to find qualified teachers to work in our schools.

- Student textbooks are in poor shape.

Working in groups, ask students to write the identified problem in the top circle of their Venn diagram. In the bottom left circle, ask them to brainstorm as many ways as they can think of to solve this problem, even if it doesn't seem possible (e.g., we could solve for the disappearance of honeybees by creating an army of robot bees to take their place). The only rule is that there is no such thing as a stupid idea—remind the students that they are looking for radical solutions. After 10 to 15 minutes of brainstorming, ask the students to choose an option to explore further. Then, in the final circle, have them write down how they might go about accomplishing it. Encourage them to think big, without regard to current technological limitations.

When the groups finish sketching out their ideas, ask them to share with the class. It might be a good idea for the entire class to start with the same problem, and compare the various ideas from different groups. Here are some ideas for adjusting this lesson plan to meet your classroom needs:

- Have students draw pictures of their radical solutions.

- Allow groups to devise their own problem to solve.

- Take time once a month to do a moonshot activity to reinforce moonshot thinking.

- Have students work alone and work in groups; compare and contrast the experience.

- After choosing a solution, have students develop a pro and con list about their plan.

- Host a moonshot fair, where student groups work in teams to solve problems and showcase the solutions.

- Incorporate moonshot thinking into a project-based learning activity.

- Ask students to interview someone about a moonshot event (e.g., ask someone who experienced the moon landing how they felt before and after; ask a parent if they would have believed iPhones were possible when they were children; etc.).

- Tackle a local problem. Bring in a community or school leader to listen to a presentation on moonshot solutions and provide feedback.

CHECK FOR UNDERSTANDING

Ask students to write about their perspectives on moonshot thinking in a journaling activity. Check group work to gauge students' demonstrated understanding of the moonshot blueprint.

AN INTERVIEW WITH FOREST KINDERGARTEN TEACHER ELIZA MINNUCCI

After watching a documentary on a forest kindergarten in Switzerland that holds open-air classes in the lush Swiss landscape, Eliza Minnucci, a teacher in Vermont, was struck with the idea that she should move her classroom to the forest, too. With the support of a forward-thinking administrator and funding from local philanthropic organizations, Minnucci, along with colleague Meghan Teachout, made her move and started Forest Fridays—one day a week when her public school kindergarten students ventured beyond the four walls of their classroom to become one with nature.

Minnucci, who had once lived off the grid without running water in a remote Athabascan village in Alaska, where she taught with a Head Start program, said that watching the documentary reminded her of the happiness and fulfillment she felt during that time in her life when she was most connected with nature. She was enamored with the idea of providing her students with a similar experience to the one that had left such an indelible impression on her.

While Minnucci's Forest Fridays were a way to connect her kids with nature, she also believed that, in many ways, the forest was a more suitable environment for her students than her classroom. Minnucci said that as a result of her young, restless charges being cooped up all day, she was already spending a great deal of time addressing behaviors like fidgeting and other manifestations of distractibility. Moving her classroom outside filled her students' innate needs to move, run, play, and shout. In addition, the forest environment allowed the students to explore their personal interests and examine and experiment with their natural surroundings.

Untethered from the classroom, Minnucci began to see incredible learning take shape. She quickly found that she could take lessons from her inside classroom—even pre-scripted math resources—and apply them to her outdoor classroom with greater effect. For example, inside the classroom, Minnucci teaches sorting by characteristics using block manipulatives of different colors and sizes. Outside, she has the students work on their sorting skills using autumn foliage, abundant in the Vermont woods. They sort by color, shape, and size, but also by the endless attributes Mother Nature provides.

"The fact that there are such a variety of answers invites more thinking, more justifying, more conversations, more vocabulary," Minnucci explains.[78] "A beginner student can sort into red, yellow, and brown, but the child next to her might see oranges and light browns, and still the next kid might have a pile for 'mottled' or 'greater than 50 percent crimson.' The depth of complexity in nature constantly communicates to a child: Keep looking! Keep thinking! Keep trying!"

This complexity the students encounter in nature also serves to bolster their growth mindsets. Minnucci noted the outdoor challenges that the kids confront are more motivating than the ones they face in the classroom. Instead of working toward extrinsic rewards, like they often did inside, the students felt empowered to tackle outdoor challenges, with a hard day's work and self-satisfaction as their only rewards. Minnucci tells about the physical struggle her kindergartners face in just getting to their outdoor space after a winter's snow.

"Hiking up the steep hill in snow up to their thighs, these five-year-olds struggle," describes Minnucci. "But there are none who just refuse to keep trying."

Indeed, the students undertake a number of demanding tasks, including dressing themselves in the appropriate winter gear, hauling heavy loads of sap on sleds, remaining motionless while observing nearby birds, and constructing sturdy shelters over a period of weeks. And beyond rising to the physical demands of outdoor life, the children learn a great deal about their inner selves in this innovative program.

Minnucci says the children develop confidence as they work to tackle challenges in the woods, and they bring that confidence back and apply it to academic pursuits in the classroom. They help care for friends who suffer scraped knees or twisted ankles. And, because there is less structure during forest time than in the traditional classroom, the kids get opportunities to develop social skills and create their own self-directed learning scenarios.

"The students quickly learn that a growth mindset in the forest is key," says Minnucci. While many of her students are comfortable in the wild environment, there are some who go into the experience with a fixed mindset. Often these are kids who don't typically experience play without the aid of toys or video games to guide the experience, but it doesn't take long before they are exploring alongside their more seasoned peers.

"The outdoors offers this environment that encourages children to pick their own appropriate challenge and work to achieve an accomplishment that is meaningful to them," says Minnucci. "[It's a] great setting to develop growth mindset because it is an endlessly complex environment."

Minnucci has gone on to develop forestkinder.org to help other teachers move their classrooms into nature. Embedded in her approach to education is the belief that teachers can serve a larger purpose beyond laying an academic foundation—namely, by doing the work of developing whole people.

"We need people who take care of each other, who are creative, who can work in diverse groups, who can express themselves clearly. We need mathematicians, programmers, scientists, nurses, lawyers, electricians, and plumbers, but we need all these people to be whole people, who can take different perspectives, tolerate hardship, work through challenges, and be creative problem solvers. We need people who recognize and value the natural resources that sustain us," says Minnucci.

Truly, every teacher like Minnucci, who makes an effort to see beyond what school is and envision what it could be, will help get us closer to that noble ambition.

CHALLENGING THE FACTORY MODEL

We get it. Not all of us can get the go-ahead to move our classrooms to the forest. Today's classrooms are not far removed from the factory model that was set up when public schools first opened in the United States so many years ago, but we can retain our moonshot thinking in an incremental environment. Your challenge is imparting the moonshot thinking to your students within a system that is not always conducive to that ethos. There are opportunities to incorporate the kind of teaching that gives students insights into how and why they learn, encourages big ideas, and promotes growth mindset, all of which can support moonshot thinkers. Here are few ideas on how to do that.

More chances	Often, schoolwork has a finality to it, but what if we were more focused on the process of learning and growing rather than completion? Allowing students more chances to demonstrate their learning, ask more questions, and build their problem-solving skills fosters a culture focused on growth. Offering practice in design thinking by exploring problems, imagining solutions, thinking the impossible, generating ideas, capturing feedback, rethinking questions and solutions, building prototypes, testing ideas, and reflecting on the process of learning teaches students to take risks and explore moonshot thinking.
Integrate technology	Technology can be a boon to teachers when used properly. Imagine if, instead of just looking at the Galapagos Islands on a map, students were able to put on a virtual headset and experience the beauty nearly firsthand? What if, instead of just learning about the dinosaurs, students could Skype with a dino dig crew? Use technology with students to encourage questioning, engage ideas, open up to new perspectives, and imagine possibilities. Our students' pool of information should be as wide as possible, never limited to the scope of one person's content knowledge or agenda.
Personalized and passionate learning	Give students opportunities to learn things at their own pace in their own way. Allowing students to pursue subjects they are passionate about can serve as a springboard for thinking big.
Celebrate awesomeness	In and around your school, celebrate teachers and students moving out of their comfort zones. Celebrate challenges, failures, and grand ideas, and join the movement to inspire moonshot thinking. Rethink, retool, and reshape what education looks likes, sounds like, and feels like in your school. Think the impossible, and get comfortable stepping out of the norm.
Network	Think beyond your classroom, your school, your state, and even your country. Seek good ideas wherever they are growing; find inspiration in educators of all stripes.
Celebrate failure	At X, people get bonuses for failing early and often. In fact, they want to know the issues with an idea so they can nix it before spending too much time on it. Attempting to take down an idea is the first step at X. If the team cannot poke holes in the plan, they know they've got the chance for an amazing moonshot.

Question, question, question	**Q.** How can you develop moonshot thinkers in your classroom?
	A. Encourage students to ask questions. A lot of questions! Why? What else? What would...? How else?
	Creating a safe place for questioning is vital to fostering moonshot thinking. Engage students in learning about different types of questioning. Offer opportunities that fuel curiosity.
	• Rapid questioning (Students ask as many questions as they can in a set amount of time: no discussing, judging, or answering during this set time.)
	• Question the questions
	• Analyze questions (open vs. closed)
	• Classify questions
Engage subject matter experts	People are doing incredible things all over the world at any given moment. Seek these people out through networking sites, ask them to Skype with your class, do an AMA (Ask Me Anything), or even send a letter. Providing authentic, relevant examples of dreamers who are out there turning their personal moonshots into reality will give students a sense of possibility in a way that reading a textbook cannot.

WRAP-UP: OUR EDUCATION MOONSHOT

We debated the best way to end this chapter on moonshot thinking, and we kept coming back to the idea that sharing our moonshot visions of education was the only appropriate ending. Using X's moonshot blueprint, we identified our big problem in education as "The traditional model of education in the United States does not serve today's learners." Then we started brainstorming big ideas that have the potential to transform the current education model for the better. Here's what we came up with:

• Education starts at home. Compulsory year-long paid maternity and/ or paternity leave should be available to every family. Free programs to provide parent education opportunities should be available in every community.

- Free, high-quality early childhood education programs should be made available to every child. Policies should exist to provide communities and families with the supportive services necessary to make early childhood education a reality for every child.

- Subsidized child care with high-quality, educated caretakers should be available in every community.

- Early childhood education professionals, healthcare professionals, parents, children, and other stakeholders should work in conjunction to determine a school readiness date. When students enter school, they would begin a personalized program in which they progress at their own pace, regardless of age. Academic and social/emotional readiness should be evaluated as students progress through their learning.

- An Individualized Learning Plan is crafted for each student. Teachers, counselors, specialists, and other school personnel should be trained to view each child as a whole person with unique needs, values, and learning goals.

- A national open educational resources database should be made available so students can access, via the Internet, the learning resources and subject matter experts relevant to their individualized learning plan.

- Education should be a valued community effort. Local organizations, businesses, and governments should create programs to offer internships, apprenticeships, and mentoring programs to help students examine different career paths, meaningfully contribute to the community, and engage in real-world work experience.

- Global-level classes taught by highly qualified master teachers should be made available via a menu of massive open online classes (MOOC) in which students can enroll. This concept will widen the pool of available classes and allows students to engage in rigorous academic learning in the fields of their choosing, rather than being limited to locally offered classes. Facilitating teachers would be available on-site to offer guidance and support in both academic and social/emotional aspects of learning. Facilitating teachers might not be versed in the subject matter of the MOOC, but rather, they would be highly skilled in the science of learning and behaviors. The facilitating teachers would help students engage in productive study, craft questions, seek out resources, connect with peers, and positively interact with the material, teacher, and fellow students.

- Grades should be eliminated. Instead of giving points and letter grades, the focus would be on collecting quantitative and qualitative data and observation of progress toward identified goals outlined in an Individualized Learning Plan. Students should also engage in classes on the "science of learning"—formally learning how to become problem solvers and critical thinkers. Students should be trained to collect data and evaluate their educational outcomes alongside the professionals.

- The teaching profession should be highly valued. Teacher preparation programs should be rigorous and, in addition to content- and age-specific preparation, teachers would be trained as learning, behavioral, and emotional scientists; teacher compensation would appropriately align with the unique and challenging nature of the job.

- Each school would have a local response team skilled in using data and observation to conduct honest self-evaluation of schoolwide performance. Instead of punitive national testing programs, the focus should be on self-improvement and growth. A national attitude of academic interdependence should be promoted, instead of competitions that pit schools against one another. Schools would work together to help one another solve problems through cooperative efforts, rather than obscuring problems, failures, and mistakes to maintain an image of success.

WHAT ARE YOUR MOONSHOT IDEAS FOR EDUCATION?

- _____

_____

_____

- _____

  _____

  _____

- _____

  _____

  _____

Sure, we could take any one of these ideas and start poking holes in them like they do at The Moonshot Factory—that idea isn't cost-effective, this one doesn't really help the students, it's unfeasible given the current education landscape, the infrastructure isn't available, etc. But moonshot thinking has to begin with possibility. The exercise of thinking big does something to the mind: It forces us to look at the situation through a new lens, it facilitates wonder and curiosity, and it opens us up to the possibility that there might be a better way. Outlining a detailed moonshot to change education is a completely different book, but, in these beginning stages, our goal is simply to engage in the exercise of big, audacious thinking.

When John F. Kennedy stood at the podium at Rice University in 1962 and told the nation that together we were going to put a man on the moon, he only had a dream. He didn't know how it would be done, he only knew that it would take the nation coming together. Kennedy knew that turning his dream into a reality wouldn't be easy, but he knew it was time to move beyond the status quo, and to do that, it was going to take all hands on deck.

"We set sail on this new sea because there is new knowledge to be gained, and new rights to be won, and they must be won and used for the progress of all people," said Kennedy. He told the crowd that audacious goals like putting a man on the moon are worthy aspirations "*not* because they are easy, *but because they are hard.*"

It's time to start thinking hard about how we can change education for the better, so why not shoot for the moon?

11

SELF-CARE AND REFLECTION

There is nothing noble in being superior to your fellow man;
true nobility is being superior to your former self.

—Ernest Hemingway

In the course of this book, we've given you lots of research, ideas, tips, and strategies for how to incorporate growth mindset into your teaching. We hope that you'll pick up a few helpful pointers and maybe drop a few bad habits, but we know that everyone who reads this book will have different takeaways. Why? Because you are each unique individuals with wildly different sets of needs, wants, and goals. If none of what we've written here resonates with you and your only takeaway is sorrow for the tree that was killed to make this book, that's okay. If this is your Holy Grail, the book you've been looking for your whole career, that's great, too. We wrote this book because embracing these big ideas and looking at teaching through a lens of growth mindset has made us better practitioners of our crafts. This is a deeply personal journey for all teachers. In the spirit of growth mindset, we insist you define success on your own terms, because if we attempt to define it for you, that's one more limitation with which you must reckon. And aren't we all just sick and tired of limitations? What success looks like for each of us is different, and only the trajectory—forward or backward—is the same. At the end of the day, only one person will determine your impact: you. You deserve the respect of self-care and the wisdom of self-reflection, and in this final chapter we'll delve into both.

YOU MATTER, TOO

Teachers spend most of the day dealing with other people's problems. Whether it's students, colleagues, parents, or administrators, in our profession we've got lots of people to answer to. Most of us got in the business of education with the understanding that other people would be involved, but particularly long and challenging days, ones that can often be mentally, physically, and emotionally draining, can leave us feeling an icky combination of overwhelmed and under-appreciated. When a teacher feels that icky feeling a bit too often, they might start to mentally pack it in. We refer to that phenomenon as burnout.

"Burnout" has a lot of negative connotations in the teaching profession; we often use it as a pejorative when describing a teacher who we think doesn't care anymore. But the truth is that we all have the capacity to get burned out many times throughout the course of our teaching career, and it's no wonder, considering the stressful nature of the job. On top of the monumental task of educating the next generation, teachers contend with all sorts of difficulties like navigating tricky relationships, dealing with unpredictable behaviors, and shouldering a heavy workload—all of which can lead to emotional exhaustion, which researchers have linked to high attrition rates among teachers.[79] What's most important is that we recognize when we're starting to show the symptoms of burnout and take steps to mediate those symptoms through self-care.

Kristen Neff, a researcher who studies self-compassion, says that people who practice self-care tend to stay "emotionally balanced in difficult situations," and outlined a three-part plan for teachers to prioritize self-care and maintain a healthy work/life balance.[80, 81]

The first component of Neff's plan is to practice self-kindness. Teachers spend their days outwardly showing kindness and compassion, but they often fail to show that same grace and love to themselves. Make sure your self-talk is positive and kind. Instead of berating yourself for a failed lesson or a negative interaction with a student, speak to yourself as you would a student who has failed in some way or made a mistake—with love and compassion.

The next part of Neff's self-compassion plan is recognizing our shared humanity. This we're-all-in-it-together attitude can help take the burden off any one teacher. Nurture compassion in yourself and among fellow teachers by focusing on the connectedness in the shared mission of education. If you've ever had one of those days where you felt like it's just you against the world, then you know that feeling isolated can have a whole host of emotional consequences. Reach out to fellow teachers to offer and ask for support, and encourage administrators to create places and spaces for teachers to share and support one another.

Finally, Neff encourages teachers to practice mindfulness. Mindfulness is simply described as an awareness of the present. For Neff, true mindfulness strikes a balance between ignoring our negative feelings and being overwhelmed by them. As she writes: "Mindfulness is a non-judgmental, receptive mind state in which one observes thoughts and feelings as they are, without trying to suppress or deny them."

Many teachers are deeply skilled at giving compassion to others, but they fail to regard their own trials with the same care. Make an effort to practice self-compassion by incorporating Neff's three components in your daily routine. Here are some ideas for how:

Journal	Taking a moment to jot down your thoughts and feelings about the day in an informal way can lead you to discoveries about your own emotions you may not have arrived at otherwise. If you feel like you don't have time to journal, considering purchasing a one-line-a-day journal to get started in a manageable way.
Meditate	In the information age, clearing our minds to meditate can initially feel very uncomfortable, but quieting thoughts and clearing headspace can serve us by promoting calmness and reflection and can lessen anxious or negative thoughts. If you're not comfortable with meditation, try finding a guided meditation to help get you started.

Connect	Sharing our burdens with one another is key to self-compassion. Consider starting a book club with fellow teachers featuring a book that will promote productive conversations about processing the physical, mental, and emotional demands of teaching. Try Neff's book, *Self-Compassion: The Proven Power of Being Kind to Yourself*, or a classic like Parker Palmer's *The Courage to Teach*. (*Psst*—A summer book club is a great way to stay connected without adding a book to your school-year workload.)
Self-care	With a job like teaching, there is no end point, so it can be really easy to overdo it. Striking a healthy work/life balance means making time for self-care. Whether you define that as treating yourself to an indulgence (like a movie, a pedicure, or a vacation) or just taking time to enjoy something you love (like reading, long walks, or a round of golf), just make the effort to be nicer to yourself.

STRATEGY SPOTLIGHT

#IWISHMY_____KNEW

"I wish my teacher knew how much I miss my dad because he got deported to Mexico when I was three years old and I haven't seen him in six years."

"I wish my teacher knew I don't have a friend to play with me."

"I wish my teacher knew sometimes my reading log is not signed because my mom is not around a lot."

Each year, Denver-area teacher Kyle Schwarz passes out sticky notes to her students and asks them to complete the phrase, "I wish my teacher knew…"[82] Reading the sometimes heart-rending responses gives Schwarz insight into her students' lives in a way that she didn't expect when she first began the exercise.

Of course, some of the responses are a bit more light-hearted.

"I wish my teacher knew how to do a backflip."

And sometimes, they offer a clear indication of what the student needs in class.

"I wish my teacher knew that I don't like it when she notices that other students are on task but when I'm on task she doesn't notice me."

Schwarz gives her students the option of writing their names or leaving their missives anonymous, or reserving it for teacher's eyes only or sharing out loud with the class. Talking to CNN, Schwarz says she feels surprised at how often her students opt to share with the entire class. She began posting some of her students' responses on Twitter with the hashtag #iwishmyteacherknew and it took off, with teachers from all over the world posting what their students wish teachers knew. Recently, Schwarz published a book, *I Wish My Teacher Knew*, about the little exercise in her third-grade Colorado classroom that was catapulted into a full-blown movement.

In her book, Schwarz says that all teachers are capable of learning how to build a collaborative classroom that fosters connection, and that forging relationships and encouraging communication with and among students are essential functions of the teacher's role. "The objectives may not be written in curriculum manuals," Schwarz writes, "but they are as essential to education as math and science."[83]

We love the idea of practicing this exercise with your students, but also thought it would be interesting to try it with teachers as well. Let's take a moment to think about your own relationships in school. What are some things that you wish others knew about you? Finish the following prompts:

I wish my principal knew...

_____

I wish my students knew...

_____

I wish my students' parents knew...

_____

I wish my colleagues knew...

_____

I wish my family knew...

_____

This exercise is a kind of simple journaling that can help identify feelings. Naming positive feelings can help us focus our gratitude; naming negative feelings is the first step to finding a remedy. So if you wrote something like, "I wish my principal knew I feel like she doesn't support me," try extrapolating on that idea and listing out reasons why.

1. She only takes a few minutes to evaluate my teaching, so it's hard to find my evaluations credible.

2. I feel like I am punished for doing a good job by having all the most challenging students placed in my classroom.

3. I have been "asked" to join three different committees. It feels like too much, especially since I have things going on with my family right now.

Now, consider whether or not there is a way to begin on a path toward remedying this problem. Is this problem one that could have a resolution? For example, a teacher feeling overtaxed by being put on a committee might write a letter explaining they are facing a lot of home commitments and ask to be replaced. Or, a teacher seeking a fair evaluation might invite administration into the classroom rather than waiting for a scheduled visit. Instead of feeling isolated and upset, finding ways to reach out in a positive way can make productive progress and lessen the negative emotion.

SELF-REFLECTION

Self-reflection is critical to understanding. When we reflect on our learning and practice, we can more effectively make improvements to our teaching, process mistakes to avoid them in the future, and uncover hidden biases or feelings. As you reflect on your teaching, you may very well recall moments that leave you shaking your head and muttering, "What was I thinking?" You are not alone. We all have those moments! We all get frustrated, make bad judgment calls, and generally do or say boneheaded things from time to time. But those things aren't nearly as destructive as the refusal to acknowledge they happened. Simply put, when you know better, you do better.

We encourage teachers to keep a journal, make a standing appointment with a mentor, videotape your teaching, or otherwise engage in reflecting on your practice. This is the essence of teaching with a growth mindset! Through this reflection, you will begin to see where improvements are needed, and can start the process of making them. If we only allow ourselves to think about our best, most successful moments as teachers, we will fail to grow.

Psychiatrist Elisabeth Kübler-Ross once said, "People are like stained-glass windows. They sparkle and shine when the sun is out, but when the darkness sets in, their true beauty is revealed only if there is a light from within."[84]

Committing to a lifetime of continued learning and improving your teaching through reflection fans the flame of your inner light. When there is a dark moment in your professional life, your light is sustained by the belief in your unending capacity for growth and change.

For our final chapter, we wanted to revisit each of the "plays" from our playbook to give you a bit more practice. Work through these exercises at your own pace. Revisit the chapter with which they are associated if you need to refresh yourself on the topics.

INTRODUCTION: THE WARM-UP

In the Introduction, we briefed you on growth mindset. In her book, *Mindset*, Carol Dweck identified five key situations in which mindset makes a big difference: challenges, obstacles, effort, criticism, and success of others.[85] Approaching these situations with either a growth or fixed orientation made a difference in the outcomes. Think about different experiences with these situations: one in which you approached the situation with a growth mindset, and one in which you approached it with a fixed mindset. What was the outcome? Compare how your outcomes differed depending on your mindset orientation.

SITUATION	GROWTH MINDSET	FIXED MINDSET	THE OUTCOME
Facing a challenge			
Overcoming an obstacle			
Having to try really hard to learn how to do something			
Receiving criticism			
Watching another person succeed			

Reflecting on how your mindset can lead to different outcomes is a meaningful practice in developing growth mindset. Mindset is present in virtually all of our decisions and actions, and being mindful of its power to lead to completely different outcomes in a given situation is the first step to becoming more adept at using mindset to improve your life.

CHAPTER 1: THE BEST WE CAN BE

In Chapter 1, we told you that the ripple effect of our impact on students is unknown and unknowable. Research has shown that childhood experiences do shape our future lives in significant ways. And even though we cannot predict how what we do with our students today will affect them in the future, we do know that helping them to understand the power they have over their lives can set them up for a lifetime of living in the growth mindset. Let's be intentional about this mission! Identify some strategies you can immediately put into practice to start incorporating growth-mindset principles in your classroom.

Growth language:
Identify how you will respond to mistakes, struggles, or failures in your classroom.

Grading:
Consider how your grading will reflect growth-mindset practices. What will you do to highlight growth?

Process praise:
How will you respond to a student making progress?

Parent communication:
Indicate how you will include parents in your growth-mindset classroom journey.

Learning:
Determine how you will incorporate lessons on brain development and plasticity.

Feedback:
How can you offer feedback that both praises effort and encourages growth?

Collaboration:
How will you share growth mindset with another educator at your school?

CHAPTER 2: BUILDING POSITIVE RELATIONSHIPS

Rita Pierson's quote bears repeating: "Every child deserves a champion, an adult who will never give up on them, who understands the power of connection, and insists they become the best they can be."[86] List your students' names in the table below and identify a specific strength, limitation, and interest of each student. Think about how you can connect wholeheartedly to each student and ways you can help them grow.

STUDENT NAME	STRENGTH(S)	LIMITATION(S)	INTEREST(S)	HOW I WILL HELP HIM/HER GROW
Example: Sam	Kind to peers and has a creative imagination	Taking on challenging tasks and being a problem solver	Basketball, reading, working with technology	I will help him learn how to problem solve by teaching him to work through computer coding tasks with a peer and independently.

STUDENT NAME	STRENGTH(S)	LIMITATION(S)	INTEREST(S)	HOW I WILL HELP HIM/HER GROW

CHAPTER 3: BRAIN TRAINING

Teaching our kids how their brains learn is a key intervention for developing growth mindsets. Students must understand that the biological processes involved in learning are capable of happening in their own heads. "I am not a math person" is a myth, because we all have billions of neurons hanging out in our brains just waiting to connect, and it's up to us to help make the connection. Further, we cannot just expect our students to get better by reading more or reviewing the study guide longer; we have to offer useful tips and strategies proven to aid in learning. If students don't know how they best learn, no amount of studying is going to make the information stick. Think about some proven memory and learning strategies like retrieval practice, and create a SMART goal for incorporating them into your classroom.

First, answer each of the following questions.

Specific—What is a specific description of the strategy you intend to use?

Measurable—How will you plan to track the progress of this goal?

Actionable—What specific steps will you take toward implementation and achievement?

Realistic—What resources and supports do you need to achieve the goal?

Timely—What is your deadline for achieving the goal?

S _____

M _____

A _____

R _____

T _____

Now, using your answers from above, write out your smart goal.

My SMART goal for incorporating evidence-based strategies proven to optimize student learning:

_____

_____

_____

_____

As you move away from traditional study methods toward evidence-based approaches to helping students truly learn information, create new goals for incorporating different strategies. This approach emphasizes your value of different learning styles and offers students an array of strategies they can use in future learning tasks.

CHAPTER 4: MISSION: METACOGNITION

Metacognition is described as understanding and having control over the higher-order thinking processes associated with learning, such as planning, strategizing, and evaluating progress. When students take this conscious approach to learning, they are able to look at their learning as a series of processes rather than a genetic gift. Further, when they understand precisely what strategies work best for them at various stages of learning, they can apply that knowledge in learning situations throughout their lives. Metacognition requires one to think and ask questions about how they learn best. Try using metacognitive questioning with yourself or in your classroom:

- Can you define the problem that you are trying to solve?

- What strategies might you use to solve this problem?

- What outcome would you like to see?

- Can you think of some steps to arrive at that outcome?

- If your first attempt at solving the problem didn't work, what obstacles prevented you from solving the problem?

- What changes could you make to improve the outcome?

- How can you use this experience to solve other problems in the future?

Metacognition is a way of looking at learning both in parts and as a whole. "Sincerely, Me" is an exercise that asks you to do just that. Imagine for a moment that you are leaving your school and a new teacher is coming to take your place. Write a letter to the new teacher explaining all about your class. What will they love most? What will be the most challenging? What advice do you have to offer?

Dear Teacher,

_____

_____

_____

_____

_____

_____

_____

_____

_____

_____

_____

Sincerely,

Me

Reflecting on our strengths and weaknesses and the specific strategies we use to maximize or overcome them is essential to becoming our best learners. It's not enough to tell students (or ourselves) that we are capable of growth; we must show them how to uncover the specific strategies that will aid in learning and development.

CHAPTER 5: AFTER THE FALL (FAILURE AS A PATH TO SUCCESS)

It's easy to have a growth mindset when you're in your comfort zone, but step one foot outside of the zone and suddenly you're far more vulnerable to fixed-mindset thinking. What do you notice about your self-talk and ability to move forward when you step out of your comfort zone? Do you fear judgment and failure? How does that fear manifest? Instead of spiraling out of control and into the fixed mindset, devise a plan for dealing with obstacles and setbacks. You will be more likely to stay in the growth-mindset zone and work through the issue.

As you begin to think of how to develop your growth-oriented classroom, think of obstacles that might stand in the way of your success. Create If/Then scenarios to help you prepare for difficult moments on your journey to growth-mindset teaching.

EXAMPLE:

If/Then: If no other teachers at my school are interested in growth-mindset teaching, then I will cultivate a community of like-minded teachers through Twitter to whom I can turn for guidance, support, and resources.

If/Then: _____

_____

If/Then: _____

_____

Struggle and failure are inevitable. It is the choices we make in the face of struggle and failure that ultimately make the difference. Value struggle as part of the learning process, normalize mistakes in your class, and don't ignore failures—dissect them! Modeling this growth-mindset approach to struggle and failure shows students that any situation can be a positive, as long as you are willing to learn from it. As Winston Churchill famously said, "Success is not final, failure is not fatal: It is the courage to continue that counts."

Growth mindset doesn't mean being perfect; it means having the courage to continue.

CHAPTER 6: THE SHAME GAME

Shame has deep implications for growth mindset. Growth mindset, at its core, is the belief that your traits and qualities can be developed over time. Think about a time that you felt shame. In that moment, you probably weren't thinking about how you could grow, change, and turn that mishap into a learning opportunity. No, you were feeling like a big worthless loser, right? Kids who are feeling shame are likely not thinking with a growth mindset, either. Which is why shame awareness is essential to the growth-mindset classroom.

Sometimes, though usually inadvertently, teachers can make students feel shame. With a roll of our eyes, a thoughtless critical comment, or frowny-face sticker on a behavior chart, there are myriad experiences students have at school that are breeding grounds for shame. Try watching yourself from the point of view of a student to examine your practices. Ask your school's AV department to borrow a GoPro camera and let your students take turns wearing it all day. Watch and listen to see if inadvertent shaming might be taking place in your classroom either from you or the students, and take steps to eliminate it.

I noticed…

_____

_____

I can ….

_____

_____

I will…

_____

_____

CHAPTER 7: THE HUMAN CONNECTION

In the course of researching this book, one fact really stood out to us: Empathy matters so much! When students feel you feeling with them, you are able to cultivate more meaningful relationships. You can take steps toward building your empathy by identifying students' feelings and trying to see the situation by remembering a time when you felt the same way. Fill in the scenarios below to help develop your empathy skills, and remember it as a way to quickly identify and empathize with students in class.

SITUATION	THE STUDENT IS PROBABLY FEELING...	A TIME I FELT THAT WAY WAS...	AN EMPATHETIC RESPONSE WOULD BE...
A student is called "fat and ugly" by another student on the playground at recess.	Hurt feelings and low self-esteem.	A friend called me stupid for getting a low score on my SAT test.	I understand it hurts when someone says an unkind thing. I want you to know those things are untrue, and that I am here to talk if you need me.
A student had to miss a field trip because his parent did not sign the permission slip.			

A student tripped at lunch and spilled her tray of food on the cafeteria floor in front of her classmates.			
A student failed an important assignment.			

It's common to want to try to repair situations by immediately going into advice mode when confronted with a problem. But resist the urge to always solve students' problems. Try to feel with your students, not for them. You may help guide them to solve the problem on their own, or you may just be a good friend in a moment of need that has no resolution. Small acts of empathy can build stronger relationships between you and your students, and modeling empathy may increase their empathetic responses toward one another.

CHAPTER 8: FOSTERING A HAPPY, COLLABORATIVE CLASSROOM

Building social capital in your classroom is key to creating a collaborative classroom. In a collaborative classroom with growth mindset at its core, everyone feels empowered to use their strengths and develop their weaknesses. Reflect on the state of collaboration in your classroom by answering the following journal prompts.

In what ways do you provide students opportunities to build relationships and connect with one another in a collaborative spirit?

_____

_____

_____

_____

_____

How might you consider explicitly incorporating role-play or social stories in your classroom to illustrate ways for students to engage with one another?

_____

_____

_____

_____

_____

Explain how you create opportunities for students to practice building social capital in the classroom.

_____

_____

_____

_____

_____

How do you address situations, conflicts, and disagreements when they arise? Do students know how to best work through disagreements?

_____

_____

_____

_____

_____

Do students understand how each learner begins in their own special place and moves at their own pace toward individual goals? How do you teach them to encourage one another in their development and growth?

_____

_____

_____

_____

_____

How do you ensure that the "superchickens" in your classroom do not get the majority of the time, attention, and resources? Ask yourself, "is my classroom an equitable learning space?'

_____

_____

_____

_____

_____

CHAPTER 9: INCREASING ENGAGEMENT

We defined engagement as student connection to a learning experience evidenced by wholehearted participation. As a multi-dimensional teacher, you should strive to inspire curiosity and wonder in your classroom every day in every student by fostering many pathways to success.

Use the single-point rubric to self-assess a lesson you have taught. How are you exceeding the criteria for engagement? What are your "not yet" areas, and how can you revise your lesson to meet the criteria?

NOT YET Areas that need improvement	CRITERIA Standards of performance	EVIDENCE How the criteria was met	ADVANCED Areas that were above and beyond
	Lesson The lesson captivates the students and sparks curiosity, as well as provides ample amounts of time for the development of additional questions and inquiry. The lesson includes collaboration time and extended learning opportunities.		
	Delivery The delivery of the lesson includes high levels of enthusiasm, excitement, and passion. Students authentically reciprocate your energy surrounding the new learning.		

NOT YET Areas that need improvement	CRITERIA Standards of performance	EVIDENCE How the criteria was met	ADVANCED Areas that were above and beyond
	Movement Students are engaged through a series of kinesthetic and tactile learning manipulatives, actions, and procedures.		

While engagement should not be confused with entertainment, one thing is clear: The passion you feel for the learning will come through in your delivery. Be excited! Be passionate! Be engaged! If you aren't engaged in and excited about the learning, then your students likely won't be, either. Challenge yourself to self-reflect and ask students to discover ways to make learning more engaging.

CHAPTER 10: MOONSHOTS

In Chapter 10, we introduced you to moonshot thinking. Moonshots are all about solving big problems with audacious solutions. As you adopt the moonshot mindset, it is critical to know your why, not just your what. If you can identify your reasons for solving a problem and why that truly matters, you can move toward your moonshot with more powerful intentions and purpose. Go back to Chapter 10 and review the moonshots you recorded. Now, write your "why"—explain why this moonshot becoming a reality would be so valuable to students and schools.

My Reasons Why

1. _____

2. _____

3. _____

Remember what President Kennedy said as he laid out his dream of putting a man on the moon? We do things not because they are easy, but because they are hard. Dare to take on the challenge of becoming a 10x teacher by working every day to turn your moonshots into realities.

NOW, CLASS, WHAT HAVE WE LEARNED?

Here we are. We've arrived at the end of our journey, or, rather, at a beginning of sorts. We hope you have been convinced of the value of incorporating growth-mindset teaching and its related non-cognitive competencies in your classroom. We hope you will be an influencer for promoting the value of character learning in your school. We hope your classroom is a place where when children enter, they feel the full weight of your belief in their boundless potential, and when they leave, they wholeheartedly believe it themselves.

Some of you might be thinking: *I am a math teacher. My job is to teach math. Why do I have to do all this extra stuff?* Because all the extra stuff, these non-cognitive competencies, matters a lot in the long run. Economist James Heckman was studying GED test takers—people who have dropped out of high school, but received the credential through the General Equivalency Development program—when he realized that even though GED recipients were cognitively equivalent to traditional high school graduates, their lack of non-cognitive skills led to much worse life outcomes.[87]

Heckman realized that getting smarter may not be the most valuable thing about the school experience. He posited that because the GED holders left school early and did not have the opportunity to cull non-cognitive soft skills associated with participating in school (perseverance, grit, work ethic, motivation, time management, self-efficacy, relationship skills) they were experiencing life outcomes more akin to high school dropouts than graduates, with higher rates of unemployment, incarceration, and drug and alcohol abuse.

"Success in life depends on personality traits that are not well captured by measures of cognition," writes Heckman in *Labour Economics*. "Conscientiousness, perseverance, sociability, and curiosity matter. While economists have largely ignored these traits, personality psychologists have studied them over the last century. They have constructed measures of them and provide evidence that these traits predict meaningful life outcomes."

As the evidence continues to mount that teaching students non-cognitive skills like growth mindset can mean positive outcomes later in life, we must begin to consider it a non-negotiable part of our craft, one that is just as valuable as the cognitive skills we aim to teach.

If that isn't a powerful enough reason for you, then consider this. When our students believe that they have the ability to get smarter and improve in any area with effort, practice, and perseverance, they benefit from a host of residual effects. No longer will they put a cap on how much they can learn, let a failure make them give up, or believe that perfection is the only acceptable outcome. When students adopt the growth mindset, they can dig into learning and truly enjoy it without fear, worry, or stress ruling the experience.

In *Mindset*, Carol Dweck wrote: "Becoming is better than being."[88]

Strive to make your classroom a place of becoming: Becoming smarter. Becoming kinder. Becoming more insightful, more curious, and more collaborative. Encourage your students to constantly work on becoming whoever it is they want to be in this world. The only thing a student should ever have to be at school is becoming. Being in your growth mindset means always developing, always learning, always becoming. Keep that thought with you, as every day, you work on becoming a better teacher than you were yesterday.

NOTES

1. Susana Claro, David Paunesku, and Carol S. Dweck. "Growth Mindset Tempers the Effects of Poverty on Academic Achievement."Vol. 113. Issue 31: 8664–8669, doi: 10.1073/pnas.1608207113.

2. Bari Walsh and Leah Shafer, "Growth Mindset and Children's Heath: Not Just for School—A Positive Mindset Has Potential to Boost Physical Well-Being, Too," *Usable Knowledge.* Harvard Graduate School of Education, https://www.gse.harvard.edu/news/uk/17/03/growth-mindset-and-childrens-health.

3. James J. Heckman and Alan B. Krueger, *Inequality in America: What Role for Human Capital Policy?* (Cambridge, MA: MIT Press, 2003).

4. David Paunesku et al., "Mind-Set Interventions Are a Scalable intervention for Academic Underachievement," *Psychological Science Online First,* April 10, 2015, doi:10.1177/0956797615571017.

5. Carol Dweck, *Mindset: The New Psychology of Success* (New York: Ballantine Books, 2006), 15–16.

6. Ibid, 16.

7. Ibid, 245.

8. Christine Gross Loh, "How Praise Became a Consolation Prize," *The Atlantic,* December 16, 2016, https://www.theatlantic.com/education/archive/2016/12/how-praise-became-a-consolation-prize/510845/.

9. Terry Goodrich, "Young White Students at Elite Colleges View Asian-Americans as More Competent than Blacks and Hispanics, Baylor Study Finds," Jan 19, 2016, http://www.baylor.edu/mediacommunications/news.php?action=story&story=164926.

10. Shane Lopez and Valerie J. Calderon, "Students Have the Will to Succeed, but Many Lack the Ways," Gallup, March 15, 2016, http://www.gallup.com/opinion/gallup/189947/students-succeed-lack-ways.aspx?g_source=&g_medium=&g_campaign=tiles.

11. Barack Obama, "Back-to-School Speech at Wakefield High," delivered Sept. 8, 2009, Arlington, VA, http://www.americanrhetoric.com/speeches/barackobama/barackobama backtoschoolspeech.htm.

12. Carol S. Dweck, "The Secret to Raising Smart Kids," *Scientific American*, January 1, 2015, https://www.scientificamerican.com/article/the-secret-to-raising-smart-kids1.

13. Carissa Romero, "What We Know About Growth Mindset from Scientific Research," Mindset Scholars Network, July 2015, http://mindsetscholarsnetwork.org/wp-content/uploads/2015/09/What-We-Know-About-Growth-Mindset.pdf.

14. Carol S. Dweck, "The Remarkable Reach of Growth Mind-Sets," *Scientific American*, January/February 2016, 38–41.

15. Education Week Research Center, "Mindset in the Classroom: A National Study of K-12 Teachers," 2016, http://www.edweek.org/media/ewrc_mindsetintheclassroom_sept2016.pdf.

16. Peter DeWitt, "Why a 'Growth Mindset' Won't Work," *Eduation Week*, July 17, 2015, http://blogs.edweek.org/edweek/finding_common_ground/2015/07/why_a_growth_mindset_wont_work.html?print=1.

17. Nadia Lopez, *Bridge to Brilliance: How One Principal in a Tough Community is Inspiring the World*, (New York: Viking, 2016), 47–50.

18. Christine Gross-Loh, "How Praise Became a Consolation Prize," *The Atlantic*, December 16, 2016, https://www.theatlantic.com/education/archive/2016/12/how-praise-became-a-consolation-prize/510845/

19. Carol Dweck, *Mindset: The New Psychology of Success* (New York: Ballantine Books, 2016) 7

20. Andie Judson, "CMS Teacher Connects to Students with Personal Handshakes," WCNC.com, February 1, 2017, http://www.wcnc.com/news/education/teacher-has-individual-handshakes-with-every-student/394516216.

21. Bridget K. Hamre and Robert C. Pianta, "Early Teacher-Child Relationships and the Trajectory of Children's School Outcomes through Eighth Grade," *Child Development*, March/April 2001, Vol. 72, Issue 2: 625–638.

22. Rita Pierson, "Every Kid Needs a Champion," video file, May 2013, https://www.ted.com/talks/rita_pierson_every_kid_needs_a_champion.

23. Richard Gunderman, "Something Is Rotten in the State of US education," *The Conversation*, May 18, 2015, https://theconversation.com/something-is-rotten-in-the-state-of-us-education-41738.

24. Wilkins, Julia, "Good Teacher-Student Relationships: Perspectives of Teachers in Urban High Schools," *American Secondary Education*, Fall 2014, Vol. 43, Issue 1.

25. C.S. Green and D. Bavelier, "Exercising Your Brain: A Review of Human Brain Plasticity and Training-Induced Learning," *Psychology and Aging*, December 2008, Vol. 23, Issue 4: 692-701, doi: 10.1037/a0014345. https://www.ncbi.nlm.nih.gov/pmc/articles/PMC2896818.

26. Carla Shatz. 1992. *Scientific American*. The Developing Brain, Vol. 267, Issue 3. 267(3); 60–67.

27. Peter C. Brown, Henry L. Roediger, Mark A. McDaniel, *Make It Stick: The Science of Successful Learning* (Cambridge, MA: Harvard University Press, 2014). 130.

28. Pooja Argarwal, *Retrieval Practice*, 2017, http://www.retrievalpractice.org.

29. Pooja Argarwal, Henry Roediger, Mark McDaniel, Kathleen McDermott, "How to Use Retrieval Practice to Improve Learning," Washington University in St. Louis, 2013, http://www.retrievalpractice.org/guide.

30. Thomas Hehir and Laura Schifter, *How Did You Get Here?: Students with Disabilities and Their Journeys to Harvard* (Cambridge, MA: Harvard Education Press, 2015).

31. Bena Kallick and Allison Zmuda, *Students at the Center: Personalized Learning with Habits of Mind,"* ASCD, January 27, 2017, 54.

32. Donna Wilson, Ph.D., "Metacognition: The Gift that Keeps Giving," Edutopia, October 7, 2014. https://www.edutopia.org/blog/metacognition-gift-that-keeps-giving-donna-wilson-marcus-conyers

33. Xiaodong lin-Siegler and Janet N. Ahn, "Even Einstein Struggled: Effects of Learning About Great Scientists' Struggles on High School Students' Motivation to Learn Science," *Journal of Educational Psychology*, 2016, Vol. 108, No. 3, 314-328 Retrieved from: http://www.apa.org/pubs/journals/releases/edu-edu0000092.pdf

34. Ibid.

35. Ibid.

36. Modeste Tchaikovsky, *The Life and Letters of Peter Ilich Tchaikovsky*, (New York: Haskell House Publishers, 1970), 281.

37. Sophia Smith, "The Japanese Art of Recognizing Beauty in Broken Things," *Make*, August 17, 2017, http://makezine.com/2015/08/17/kintsugi-japanese-art-recognizing-beauty-broken-things.

38. Gail Sullivan, "New Kid at School Forced to Wear 'Shame Suit' for Dress Code Violation," *The Washington Post,* September 5, 2014, https://www.washingtonpost.com/news/morning-mix/wp/2014/09/05/new-kid-at-school-forced-to-wear-shame-suit-for-dress-code-violation/?utm_term=.7128ec54af41.

39. Brené Brown, "Public Shaming is a Better Example of "If It Feels Good—Do It" than Teen Pregnancy," March 20, 2013, http://brenebrown.com/2013/03/20/2013320meuitdwaubpgr9qt1xanm3fwwa0sjo.

40. Brené Brown, "Teachers, Shame, and Worthiness: A Lesson Learned," September 29, 2013, http://brenebrown.com/2013/09/29/teachers-shame-worthiness-lesson-learned.

41. Nikki Sabiston, "Why I Will Never Use a Behavior Chart Again." *Teaching in Progress,* October 2012, http://www.teachinginprogress.com/2012/10/why-i-will-never-use-behavior-chart.html.

42. Nikki Sabiston (elementary school teacher), in discussion with the author, December 31, 2016.

43. Brené Brown, "Listening to Shame," video file, March 2012, https://www.ted.com/talks/brene_brown_listening_to_shame.

44. Ann Monroe, "Shame Solutions: How Shame Impacts School-Aged Children and What Teachers Can Do to Help," The Educational Forum, January 7, 2009, Vol. 73, Issue 1, 2008: 58–66, http://dx.doi.org/10.1080/00131720802539614.

45. Brené Brown, *Daring Greatly: How the Courage to Be Vulnerable Transforms the Way We Live, Love, Parent, and Lead* (New York Gotham Books, 2012), 192.

46. Mary Pipher, *Reviving Ophelia: Saving the Selves of Adolescent Girls*, Media Education Foundation, http://www.mediaed.org/transcripts/Reviving-Ophelia-Transcript.pdf.

47. Margaret Mead, "Frequently Asked Questions about Mead/Bateson," Institute for Intercultural Studies, http://www.interculturalstudies.org/faq.html.

48. Carl Ransom Rogers, *The Carl Rogers Reader,* (New York: Houghton Mifflin Harcourt, 1989), 225.

49. Saul McLeod, "Carl Rogers," *Simply Psychology*, https://www.simplypsychology.org/carl-rogers.html.

50. Brené Brown, "The Power of Vulnerability," video file, June 2010, https://www.ted.com/talks/brene_brown_on_vulnerability.

51. Mariah Flynn, "Teachers Can Reduce Suspensions by Practicing Empathy," *Greater Good*, May 26, 2016, http://greatergood.berkeley.edu/article/item/teachers_can_reduce_suspensions_by_practicing_empathy.

52. Editorial Board of *The New York Times*, " The School-to-Prison Pipeline," *New York Times*, May 30, 2013: A.22.

53. United States Department of Education Office for Civil Rights, "Civil Rights Data Collection, Issue Brief No. 1," March 2014, http://ocrdata.ed.gov/downloads/crdc-school-discipline-snapshot.pdf.

54. Matt Davis, "Restorative Justice: Resources for Schools," *Edutopia*, October 4, 2013, https://www.edutopia.org/blog/restorative-justice-resources-matt-davis.

55. Schott Foundation, "Restorative Practices: Fostering Healthy Relationships and Promoting Positive Discipline in Schools," March 2014, http://www.otlcampaign.org/sites/default/files/restorative-practices-guide.pdf.

56. PERTS, "Can a Shift in Mindset Reduce Suspensions?" *Medium*, June 28, 2016, https://medium.com/learning-mindset/can-a-shift-in-mindset-reduce-suspensions-30ef50912015.

57. Ibid.

58. William M. Muir and David Sloan Wilson, "When the Strong Outbreed the Weak: An Interview with William Muir," The Evolution Institute, July 11, 2016, https://evolution-institute.org/article/when-the-strong-outbreed-the-weak-an-interview-with-william-muir.

59. Margaret Heffernan, "Forget the Pecking Order at Work," video file, May 2015, https://www.ted.com/talks/margaret_heffernan_why_it_s_time_to_forget_the_pecking_order_at_work.

60. Alix Spiegel, "Teachers' Expectations Can Influence How Students Perform," NPR, September 17, 2012, http://www.npr.org/sections/health-shots/2012/09/18/161159263/teachers-expectations-can-influence-how-students-perform.

61. Walter Mischel and Ebbe B. Ebbesen, "Attention in Delay of Gratification," *Journal of Personality and Social Psychology*, Volume 16, Issue 2, October 1970, 329-337, doi:10.1037/h0029815.

62. Jacoba Urist, "What the Marshmallow Test Really Teaches About Self-Control," *The Atlantic*, September 24, 2014, https://www.theatlantic.com/health/archive/2014/09/what-the-marshmallow-test-really-teaches-about-self-control/380673.

63. "The Marshmallow Study Revisited," University of Rochester, October 11, 2012. http://www.rochester.edu/news/show.php?id=4622.

64. Lauren Schiller and Christina Hinton, "It's True: Happier Students Get Higher Grades," July 30, 2015, https://theconversation.com/its-true-happier-students-get-higher-grades-41488.

65. Zachary Jason, "Bored Out of Their Minds," *Harvard Ed* Magazine, Winter 2017, https://www.gse.harvard.edu/news/17/01/bored-out-their-minds

66. Jal Mehta and Sarah Fine, "Why the Periphery Is Often More Powerful Than the Core," *HarvardEd.Magazine*,Winter2017,http://www.gse.harvard.edu/news/ed/17/01/why-periphery-often-more-powerful-core.

67. Lory Hough, "Beyond Average," *Harvard Ed. Magazine*, Fall 2015, http://www.gse.harvard.edu/news/ed/15/08/beyond-average.

68. Ibid.

69. Ibid.

70. Jarene Fluckinger, "Single Point Rubric: A Tool for Responsible Student Self-Assessment," *Teacher Education Faculty Publications*, 2010, http://digitalcommons.unomaha.edu/tedfacpub/5

71. Kathy Liu Sun, "There's No Limit: Mathematics Teaching for a Growth Mindset," Dissertation, 2015, Stanford University, Graduate School of Education, https://purl.stanford.edu/xf479cc2194

72. George Slavich, "On Becoming a Teacher of Psychology," 2006, University of California at Los Angeles, http://uclastresslab.org/pubs/Slavich_TeachingAutoBio_2006.pdf

73. Jo Boaler, "Multidimensional Mathematics," YouCubed, https://www.youcubed.org/multidimensional-mathematics.

74. Shaun Killian, "8 Strategies Robert Marzano and John Hattie Agree On," The Australian Society for Evidence Based Teaching, June 17, 2015, http://www.evidencebasedteaching.org.au/robert-marzano-vs-john-hattie.

75. "Tips From Dr. Marzano: The Highly Engaged Classroom," *Marzano* Research, https://www.marzanoresearch.com/resources/tips/hec_tips_archive#tip15

76. Sir Ken Robinson, 2010, "Bring On the Learning Revolution!" (speech), TED talk video recording, https://www.ted.com/talks/sir_ken_robinson_bring_on_the_revolution

77. X, "What We Do," x.company/about.

78. Eliza Minnucci (elementary school teacher), in discussion with the author, January 7, 2017.

79. Costas N. Tsouloupas, Russell L. Carson, Russell Matthews, Matthew J. Grawitch, and Larissa K. Barber, "Exploring the Association Between Teachers' Perceived Student Misbehavior and Emotional Exhaustion: The Importance of Teacher Efficacy Beliefs and Emotion Regulation," *Education Psychology*, Vol. 30, Issue. 2, 2010, do: 10.1080/01443410903494460.

80. Vicki Zakrzewski, "How Self-Compassion Can Help Prevent Teacher Burnout," *Greater Good,* September 11, 2012, http://greatergood.berkeley.edu/article/item/self_compassion_ for_teachers.

81. Kristin Neff, "The Three Elements of Self-Compassion," Self-Compassion.org, http://self-compassion.org/the-three-elements-of-self-compassion-2.

82. Jamie Gumbrecht, "#IWishMyTeachersKnew shares students' heartbreaks, hopes," CNN.com, April 20, 2015, http://www.cnn.com/2015/04/17/living/i-wish-my-teacher-knew-kyle-schwartz-schools-feat/index.html

83. Kyle Schwartz, *I Wish My Teacher Knew: How One Question Can Change Everything for Our Kids,* (Boston, MA: Da Capo Press, 2016), 15.

84. Elisabeth Kubler-Ross, Foundation, "50 Quotes by Elisabeth Kubler-Ross," http://www.ekrfoundation.org/quotes.

85. Carol Dweck, *Mindset: The New Psychology of Success* (New York: Ballantine Books, 2006), 245.

86. Rita Pierson, "Every Kid Needs a Champion," video file, May 2013, https://www.ted.com/ talks/rita_pierson_every_kid_needs_a_champion.

87. James J. Heckman, John Eric Humphries, Nicholas S. Mader, "The GED," National Bureau of Economic Research, June 2010, http://www.nber.org/papers/w16064.pdf.

88. Carol Dweck, *Mindset: The New Psychology of Success* (New York: Ballantine Books, 2006), 25.

INDEX

W

"We're-all-in-it-together" attitude, 156

"What's my face?" game, 102

White, Barry, Jr., and positive relationships, 30, 31

Williamson, Marianne, quoted, 136

Women, and empathy, 111

Work ethic, 69

Writing project, and empathy exercises, 105

X

X (formerly Google X), and moonshot thinking, 137–40, 142, 143; website, 138, 139

Z

Zmuda, Allison, and learning strategies/styles, 57

ACKNOWLEDGMENTS

Thank you to our husbands, Matt and Jared, for helping pick up the slack at home while we worked on this book. Your support makes it all possible. Thank you to our children—Abbigail, Addison, Abbott, Bodhi, and Lila—for your patience and support. You truly are our inspiration!

To Eliza Minnucci (forestkinder.org), Nikki Sabiston (teachinginprogress.com), Pooja Agarwal (retrievalpractice.org), Cindy Moulin, and Shelley Sopha—thank you for sharing your ideas, stories, and strategies with us. This book is better thanks to your contributions. And, of course, to Carol Dweck and all the researchers who work tirelessly to contribute to the canon that seeks to improve both the craft of teaching and the act of learning.

Much of this book was written in a tiny room in the back of Holton Tire and Service in Holton, Kansas. Thank you to Clint and Kelly Brock for providing a quiet space, free WiFi, and comfy recliners. It was exactly what we needed!

Special thanks to our many friends and family, who are an endless source of support and encouragement: Aryannah, Mackenzie, Roy, Carolyn, David, Sharon, Bob, Gary, Cindy, Jake, Stevie, Sam, Lori, Inga, Joe, Norah, and Amy.

Thank you to our colleagues in education, who are a constant source of support and inspiration for our writing. Your posts, shares, tweets, chats, and book studies have inspired us to keep writing and sharing with the education community. We are so honored to be part of a profession packed with inventive, resourceful people who are incredibly generous with their time and ideas.

Thank you to our home bases for teaching and learning—USD 336 in Holton, Kansas and Greenbush Southeast Kansas Education Service Center—and all the students, teachers, and staff of these organizations who come together each day to fulfill the honorable mission of high-quality public education.

And, finally, thank you to our editor, Casie Vogel, and the team at Ulysses Press. We are so thankful for your support, guidance, and dedication to helping us create and distribute a final product that makes us so proud.

—A.B. and H.H.

ABOUT THE AUTHORS

Annie Brock, coauthor of *The Growth Mindset Coach*, is a library media specialist and former English language arts teacher. She graduated with a degree in journalism and mass communications from Kansas State University and earned her teaching credentials through Washburn University. Annie previously authored *Introduction to Google Classroom*. She lives in Holton, Kansas, with her husband, Jared, and their two children.

Heather Hundley is director of curriculum and assistant elementary principal at USD 336 in Holton, Kansas. Heather has an elementary education degree from Washburn University and master's degrees in education and in school leadership from Baker University. She has served as a supervisor for pre-service teachers, guest lecturer at Washburn University, and instructional support specialist for Greenbush Southeast Kansas Education Service Center. Heather previously coauthored *The Growth Mindset Coach*. She lives in Holton with her husband Matt and their three children.